WHO'S PULLING YOUR STRINGS?

WHO'S PULLING YOUR STRINGS?

HOW TO STOP BEING MANIPULATED BY YOUR OWN PERSONALITIES

LOUIS PROTO

Foreword by Hal Stone

THORSONS PUBLISHING GROUP

First published 1989

British Library in Publication Data

Proto, Louis
Who's pulling your strings?
1. Self-realisation
I. Title
158'.1

ISBN 0-7225-1732-7

Published by Thorsons Publishers Limited, Wellingborough, Northamptonshire, NN8 2RQ, England

Printed in Great Britain by Billing & Sons Limited, Worcester
Typeset by MJL Limited, Hitchin, Hertfordshire

1 3 5 7 9 10 8 6 4 2

CONTENTS

FOREWORD

We live in a time when the evolution of human consciousness is becoming an increasingly important issue to more and more people. As each of us begins this journey, the journey of our own individual consciousness process, we start to become aware of our inner life and, as we do so, we notice that an amazing amount of activity goes on within us. We discover all kinds of interesting feelings, thoughts, intuitions and bodily sensations that we never knew existed until we began to focus on them.

One of the most surprising discoveries that we can make in this process of self-exploration is the realization that we are made of many parts or selves. These parts are like an inner family of people, each member of which behaves, acts, feels and talks like a real person. Each has its own life story, feelings and emotions. Each has a philosophy of life. Most of them seem to know exactly how we should behave in the world. As Louis Proto puts it so beautifully in the title of his book, each is happy to take its turn pulling our strings and determining who we are and how we behave in life.

How is it that we develop this family? We are born into this world as totally helpless infants and must be cared for if we are to survive. We do this by developing a variety of inner selves that protect our basic vulnerability and ensure that we get the care that we need. The first of these selves to develop is the Protector-Controller. It is this self that looks about us and figures out how we might best protect ourselves. Its basic task is to protect us from being hurt either physically or psychologically. Once it determines the best course of action to take, it then controls our behaviour so that we will not be hurt. It is the first of our inner family to develop and it usually determines which members are to be favoured and which are to be disowned.

As we continue our growing up process, other selves develop and are added to this inner family. As young children we might realize that mother likes us to smile. So we begin to smile more frequently, not just because we want to smile, but because we know that it pleases Mum. So our Pleaser is born, and pleasing becomes more important than our natural tendency to smile. The Pleaser then joins the Protector-Controller to help us to move through life safely. Our fathers might be especially happy when we get good grades and when we behave well at school. We then develop a Pusher, a hard-working self, who requires us to work all the time so that Dad will be happy with us. A Perfectionist might also develop, one that will do everything properly and perfectly so that everyone in the world, we hope, will admire us and be pleased with our efforts. At some point in our development, an Inner Critic comes alive. This Critic will criticize us for not following the rules of the other selves who determine how it is we *should* be in the world. So it is that we develop our inner family, one that is specifically ours, but which bears some similarity to the neighboring families as well.

The range of selves that live inside of us is very large indeed. Many approaches to growth and healing work with these different selves in one way or another. Each self represents a distinctively different kind of energy and, in fact, we often refer to them as 'energy patterns'. There is no self that is inherently good or bad. Each makes its own special contribution to the unique being that we are in the world. It is very basic to our thinking that these widely varying energies are not to be judged. For example, if someone is very identified with more conservative and contracted self or selves, it is quite common that people favour and support the development of a free spirit and more expansive self. From our perspective, neither the more conservative nor the more expansive self is 'good' or 'bad'. Both represent a natural way of being that we need to live a full and effective life. They represent opposite ends of a continuum of energy and our task is to develop an aware ego that can both embrace and learn to balance these very different selves. If we identify with the conservative, then we are forever at odds with people that are identified with the liberal or expansive side. If we identify with the liberal, then we are forever at odds with those people who are more identified with the conservative self. It is only when we can embrace opposites that we have real choice in life. The more one learns about these different selves, the less judgemental one becomes about them.

One of the things that we learn about these selves, as Louis Proto has discussed in considerable detail in his book, is that the people we judge and hate in life are in fact reflections of our disowned selves. This is a remarkable piece of information to have available because it can help each of us to learn a great deal about ourselves. If you can't stand people who are very domineering, if you feel very angry and judgemental towards them, then we know automatically that there is a part of yourself that is disowned, that is kept unconscious and unavailable to you. Whatever we disown, life brings to us in some way. We may marry someone with those qualities. One of our children may live out those qualities. We may work with someone who has those qualities. Whatever the case, these situations create conditions of great stress for us until we are able to step back and see that the person we judge and hate is in fact a reflection of our own disowned self system. At this point, we recognize the other person as being a teacher for us at some level. This does not mean that we have to identify with the traits that we hate or become like that person. It simply means that we have to learn to honour that person and those traits. We must learn that they are also a part of us that has been kept unconscious by the stronger parts of us (the primary selves) with which we have identified in the growing up process.

On a global level the implications of this are really quite staggering. How do we help to create peace in the world unless we can begin to recognize that our enemies, the people we judge and hate, are to some extent reflections of our own psychology? We cannot embrace the world until we can embrace ourselves. Real choice in dealing with people can only come when we have some awareness and experience and appreciation of these diverse characters that live within each of us.

There are some very important decisions being made in the world today. As our planet shrinks, these decisions have far-reaching political, economic and ecological implications. We are living in a era that has enormous potential — both for growth and destruction. The more conscious the decisions, the better it will be for all of us. An awareness of selves is essential to choice and conscious decision making. How often it happens that someone's feelings are hurt and out of this hurt springs the other side; righteousness, power, dogmatism and eventually action springing from these kinds of feelings. To embrace ourselves is to embrace our planet. That is the real meaning of this book.

Louis Proto has used his rich background in history, literature, mythology and psychology to bring us a lively and literate look at this inner family. In an exciting and straightforward way, he tells us about many of its members and shows us how they operate in the world. He shows us how he views them, pointing out the assets and liabilities that each family member represents for us. No one can read this book without coming away from it deeply enriched and with a much greater awareness of who within us is, indeed, pulling the strings.

Dr Hal Stone
California
1988

ACKNOWLEDGEMENTS

The author wishes to thank Drs Hal Stone and Sidra Winkelman, not only for generously granting permission to quote from their Voice Dialogue Manual *Embracing Our Selves* (New World Library), but because, without their vision, this book could not have been written. It is therefore with gratitude, as well as with love, that it is dedicated to them, though they may not necessarily agree with all of the ideas expressed in it.

WHO'S PULLING YOUR STRINGS?

Have you ever wondered why you think, feel and react the way you do? Why for example, you

- chose your career or job
- are happy in it or not
- chose your husband, wife or lover
- vote the way you do
- sometimes get confused when you have to make a decision
- work harder than you need to
- find it hard to relax
- can't say 'no'
- find it hard to assert yourself
- sometimes feel depressed or irritable without obvious reason
- feel frustrated, in a rut
- lack confidence
- lose your temper
- act 'out of character'
- feel anxious or vulnerable
- keep repeating the same patterns in relationships
- fall in love
- fall out of love
- like certain types of people, can't stand others
- have the dreams you do
- enjoy the films you do
- attract the experiences you do?

It was Freud who first showed us just how much we are all the time being influenced by forces operating from a place in us below the level of consciousness which he called the subconscious. He even seemed at times to suggest that there are no 'accidents'. At some level a part of you knows what you are doing when you make a 'Freudian slip' — because it made you do it. It could be a slip of the tongue, forgetting an appointment or being late for one, or 'accidentally' spilling a cup of tea over the person who made that bitchy remark ten minutes ago. Whichever part of you it was (and in each of the above examples it was probably a different part) it got you to do what *it* wanted you to do.

There are many more more or less hidden parts to us than we imagine. They cause us to do things mechanically, repetitively, often without really wanting to or really knowing why. Sometimes different parts of us are in conflict, as when we experience 'mixed feelings' or get confused by different voices within us urging quite contradictory courses of action when we have an important decision to make. It is commonplace to hear people on these occasions declaring that 'a part of me wants to do this, another part of me doesn't.' Sometimes, to our uncomprehending shame, we may even find ourselves acting against our best intentions. As Saint Paul complained: 'For the good I would I do not; but the evil which I would not, that I do.' Alice in Wonderland was just as perplexed about why she should feel the way she did, when she did, as Saint Paul was about why he continually found himself doing what he knew he shouldn't be doing.

> Let me think; was I the same when I got up this morning? I almost think I can remember feeling a little different. But if I'm not the same, the next question is, Who in the world am I?

A very good question, and one that through the ages has exercised many more sophisticated minds than Alice's.

For what makes people 'tick', the paradoxes, contradictions and conflicts in human nature, are a large part of religion, philosophy and economics, the stock-in-trade of novelists and dramatists, the concern of psychotherapy. Psychotherapy in particular has provided us with some very good models for coming up with a few answers. Our investigation of the sources of at least some of the hidden string-pulling from the Unconscious follows the model (described in the Appendix) evolved by Dr Hal Stone and Dr Sidra Winkelman for getting to know our selves better. Often, to the extent that we remain unaware of these selves, they control us, just as if we were puppets on a string. When this particular string is pulled we always get angry; when others are tugged we always find ourselves feeling jealous, anxious, embarrassed — or anything else *ad infinitum*.

We human beings are more than just the sum of the total of our parts and will always remain ultimately as mysterious as the place we came from and to which we will return in the end. That said, there is some enlightenment to be gained (and, I hope, some enjoyment), from exploring more deeply who we are while we are here. To know our selves, to be them more and to be more of them, is perhaps what we are all really here for. Not only that, but if you know which part you are playing at any one time, it is easier to keep your act together.

INTRODUCING OUR SELVES

PUBLIC FACES, PRIVATE PARTS

Have you ever considered how many different roles you play within your own family? How many of these, for example, are you?

- parent
- spouse
- grandparent
- son or daughter
- uncle or aunt
- in-law
- cousin
- nephew or niece?

Whenever you are with any member of your family you will slip naturally and easily into the different way of relating that you have with each one. You will be quite a different person, for example, when you are having afternoon tea with your mother than when you are in bed with your spouse (at least, one hopes so), or trying to get the children off to school in the morning. You may not feel exactly the same each time you are with your mother, spouse or children (though it is possible, if the jokes are to be believed, that you may with your mother-in-law), but each would be surprised if you were to depart noticeably from the usual range of responses which they have become accustomed to expect from you. They might think you were rather odd or not feeling well, and would probably ask you what was the matter.

This is because what they are picking up is that you are acting 'out of character', expressing yourself or relating with a type of energy that does not fit with this particular family role. Depending, for example, on whether you are letting them stay up to watch television or ordering them to bed, your children may see you as Good Parent or Bad Parent. But, either way, you have not stepped out of a parenting role. The sort of energy that goes with this role is more or less affectionate, nurturing and protective, more or less controlling. And, within these parameters, consistent.

When you leave the house in the morning to go to work you leave your family roles (or if you will pardon the expression, your private parts) behind and prepare yourself to assume your work roles. What these particular ways of being are depends on the type of work you do and your job status. And, depending on the job, a different type of role will be expected from you, expressing a different quality of energy. Some jobs demand close attention to detail, care and concentration, for example, surgery, accountancy or research. Others call for extroversion and projection of an image: acting, for example, or politics (which at times seems very much like acting). Yet others demand from you the ability to give or to carry out orders, to work as part of a team, or to take responsibility for working on your own with little or no support. All different ways of being, different types of energy.

Not only do different jobs call on different skills and energies, but many of them demand that we present a definite image while we are doing them. Jung called this the *persona*, the mask which, like actors in ancient Greek plays, we put on to face our audience and project a certain type of character. This is convenient all round, for it helps us to become who we are supposed to be, the role we are supposed to be playing — and the professional mask makes it easier for others to recognize who we are and to relate appropriately to us in that role. It is usually either embarrassing, disturbing or comical if the mask slips unexpectedly and we are suddenly confronted with another aspect of the person; if, for example, the politician shows uncertainty or vulnerability, the circus clown attacks the ringmaster for real, or our analyst suddenly throws a tantrum when we are paying for the privilege of throwing our own. We may suspect that there is more to people than the professional image they present us with. What is unsettling is that there is an appropriate time and place for these other ways of being to pop out, but this wasn't it.

THE EGO

There is a central distinction between that part of us which, like Alice, experiences our changing moods and is aware enough of them to ask the questions: 'Who in the world am I?' — and the moods themselves. Unless you are schizophrenic or, like the woman in *Three Faces of Eve*, a multiple personality, you will be very familiar with your everyday 'I' which is in touch with changing circumstances in your environment, capable of adjusting to it and exercising choice and making decisions. This is what Freud called the Ego (which might be egotistical in some people but is not necessarily so), the part of you that not only thinks, feels and acts, but is capable, more or less, of being aware also that it does so.

The importance of realizing that we are not our moods but the *experiencer* of them makes all the difference to how we live our lives, conduct our relationships and express ourselves in the world. To the extent that our moods are allowed to control us they manipulate us. Alice is not the only one who gets confused by her changing feelings, pushed around by them: so, at times do we all. For they propel us, as they did Saint Paul, in directions in which we perhaps would rather not go, making us feel uncomfortable and *driven*. We may feel depressed, irritable, anxious without knowing why, needy without having a clue as to what we really want. We react in stereotyped and repetitive ways to the same situations when they arise, slavishly following the scripts imposed by our heredity, environment and expectations. We *always* get angry when this particular string is pulled, always walk out of a relationship when we feel a tug on that one.

There is nothing wrong with anger as such, or knowing when you have had enough. It all depends on the circumstances, the appropriateness, your in-touchness with the realities of the situation. You may be totally justified in walking out on your partner if he or she is really behaving abominably. The point is not what you do, but whether you give yourself any choice in the matter, *whether you are responding or merely reacting*. In other words, whether you can choose *not* to act out whatever it is you may be thinking or feeling. And it is not only a question of giving yourself more space to be the way *you* want to be rather than the way your internal string-pullers manipulate you into being. Sometimes, indeed, especially if they are angry with you for not taking them seriously, the string-pullers might be trying to steer you in directions that could land you in trouble, in hospital, or jail. Some of them, like the exploiter Stromboli (Pinocchio's puppet-master) are harsh and will drive you to the point of collapse. Others could push you 'over the top' so that you damage yourself or other people. Many of them don't care about considerations like appropriateness, or even about what the other puppeteers are trying to get you to do. Which means that at times you will feel pulled in different directions at the same time, experiencing conflict, indecision, confusion. Understandably, since it is not clear which way you are supposed to move. Too many double messages and double-binds could drive you crazy.

When we talk about 'changing moods' we are really talking about different states of feeling-energy. There must be few people who have not experienced the feeling-tone that goes with jealousy, for example, or with vulnerability. There are few more unpleasant states of feeling than when these two strings are being pulled at the same time. It is a great help at times like this if one can be in touch with the vulnerability as well as the jealous anger. The more aware one is of exactly *what* one is feeling the more choice one has as to whether to vent the anger or share the vulnerability. How one's partner responds to either is in the lap of the Gods, but at least one feels less driven, more in control of oneself and the situation. For it is giving yourself a *choice* as to whether to act out or not (and *what* to act out) that gets you off the hook, at least temporarily. But in order not to get hooked again next time a similar situation arises takes even more awareness. The puppet-master who this time pulled your string marked 'jealousy' is still there behind the scenes ready to hook you into your next performance right on cue, perhaps at the next party to which you, your partner and the Offending Party are invited.

You cannot destroy any part of you, any of these energies within you, however much you would rather they were not there. We shall be describing in a later chapter the dire results of trying to disown any of these energies life has given you. Try to understand them, however, you can — and the more you understand them, of course, the more you understand yourself — or rather your selves that make you think, feel and act the way you do. Understanding more, you will judge yourself less, for you will see how always, however it looks from the outside, your psyche is doing the best it can to try and meet your needs and to cope with pressures both from within and without — to keep you, in fact, alive and sane. You will be kinder to yourself, less harsh — and be more aware of the part of you that tends to be harsh on yourself because it has been taught to be so. Dealing harshly with yourself forestalls, perhaps, the harder ordeal of having to bear that harshness coming from other quarters.

Being kinder to yourself will rub off on others, for we tend to treat others the way we treat ourselves. You will be more interested in looking behind what they do to sense the place they are coming from, the part of them that is at that moment pulling *their* strings, making them behave in this particular fashion. And, as you become more comfortable with the parts of yourself that up till now you have been taught to condemn as 'bad' or 'ugly', you will feel less threatened or judgemental when they appear before you in others. For every judgement we make about another is in fact an indication of our own boundaries, refusal to acknowledge that this particular form of energy is a potential part of us too. As we shall be seeing, the more you resist a certain type of energy, the more it will fight to be acknowledged, and the more it will tend to manifest in your life. Your resistance to it will attract the same sorts of experiences over and over again to you like a magnet. The energy that you deny in yourself will haunt you, both in real life and in your dreams.

If you are in touch with your motivations, with your needs, with your blind spots and the ways you tend to go 'over the top' given half a chance, your Ego, the part of you that has the job of making decisions, is better equipped for avoiding disastrous false moves and errors of judgement. It has more intelligence (literally) to go on — and therefore acts more intelligently, more appropriately to the external situations with which it finds itself having to cope. The more aware your Ego becomes of the different selves within you, the less it is at the mercy of these internal puppet-masters and compelled willy-nilly to dance to their string-pulling. You will experience more freedom, more choice and more direction, for you will be better able to work with these energies to bring more quality into your life, instead of being pulled about by them, often in different directions at the same time. You move in fact from the position of Victim to being more in charge of your life and more truly responsible for what you put into it and what you get out of it. Which is what society (and the law) expect from us anyway.

SUBPERSONALITIES — THE PEOPLE INSIDE YOU

What we have been referring to as string-pulling puppet masters are in fact constellations of energy in the unconscious which predispose us to think, feel and react in well-defined and recurring ways. Psychoanalysts refer to them as complexes, patterns of behaviour, or archetypes. To the extent that they stay in the unconscious they are not only inaccessible to any efforts of the Ego to change them (assuming that the Ego is even aware of them), but may even sabotage those efforts. Split off from our awareness, they behave in fact rather like autonomous subselves, and are therefore known as subpersonalities. And this is a very good name for them, for they do in fact behave remarkably like real people inside us.

Just like real people, they come in all shapes and sizes. The ones we identify with and think of as 'ourselves' are in fact only the 'heavyweights' — the most developed (sometimes overdeveloped) of our selves that get a lot of exercise because we rely on them so much to get us through life. There are in fact more selves or subpersonalities in us than the ones we identify with, or even are aware of, and in the chapters that follow we shall be identifying some (certainly not all) of the most commonly found. Other subpersonalities, which we have not got around to developing, are 'thin', for they do not get much chance to come out and, metaphorically speaking, flex their muscles through being expressed in our lives. Some subpersonalities are old, wise in the ways of the world and tough as old boots: these are your power subpersonalities. Others are as young and innocent as children: exquisitely (sometimes painfully) sensitive and vulnerable. Yet others, potential selves, are still in embryo, waiting to be born when the time is ripe and if you will allow it.

Like any other group of individuals they are a mixed bag and include all sorts of characters, the 'good', the 'bad' and the 'ugly'. How you relate to these parts of yourself depends on how you have been educated or conditioned to view them. The parts you have been taught to regard as 'good' you will embrace, identify with, and like to think of as 'you'. You will nourish them and be proud to show them to others. The ones you have been taught to think of as 'bad' or 'ugly' you will try to hide, be ashamed of and reject, and hope nobody else discovers that, 'deep down', you are really 'like that'. For that is where you will push these disowned subpersonalities, deeper down into the unconscious where they cannot be seen. But they are ALL you, and, like all of us, want to be seen and heard, acknowledged and respected, allowed to sing their song.

Each subpersonality has a function to perform for you — that is why it is there. Basically, once again like people, they fall into two groups, the ones who tend to be conservative and the ones who tend to be more radical. In Freudian terms, the equivalent classification would be between the ones that are on the side of the Superego and those that are more Id-orientated. Among the first group are the parts of you that appreciate order and security, are cautious, critical (perhaps even suspicious) and form a large part of your 'commonsense'. They enable you to look after yourself, to stay on the right side of the law, to earn your living and to 'fit in' with others. Their survival value is obvious and the fact that you are still around testifies to the fact that they have been serving you well. They might well, however, find themselves from time to time in conflict with the parts of you that fall into the other, more liberal, category — the parts of you that are more geared to freedom, love and self-expression, to excitement and having fun, to exploring your own creativity and being willing to follow wherever life is taking you. Without these parts your life would be dull, stagnant, joyless: a desert, devoid of imagination, romance, adventure or fulfilment.

To consider these various parts of ourselves as if they were different people inside us is a useful model for understanding our selves. For these subpersonalities, like all of us, have each their own way of seeing, their own motivations, desires, needs. And, providing they are allowed to contribute what it is they specialize in and can bring to us, they will continue to function in our best interests *as they see them*. They are a part of the Whole (us), and make us who we are, together with our Ego awareness. The latter, this 'I' so familiar to all of us as our 'everyday mind', is rather in the position of the Boss with the job of keeping an eye on the whole team as well as on the market-place (outside realities). In response to internal pressure or in the event of a dispute, the Boss may have to arbitrate between conflicting demands for action and to make decisions on the grounds of what is realistic and appropriate at that time. If subpersonalities feel their case has been fairly heard by the Ego Decision-Maker who is their executive and understand the expediency of the decision, they will go quietly back to work, or at least not strike or resort to drastic forms of protest to get their policies implemented. If on the other hand, a subpersonality feels unfairly treated, ignored and excluded from the Boss's advisory council it may well turn sour and disgruntled, or even to sabotage.

What we are really talking about here, of course, is the advisability of listening to all the parts of ourselves instead of only the few we are identified with and think of as 'us'; of being honest with ourselves as to our true motivations and daring to acknowledge our real needs; of trying to understand and come to terms with the parts of us we feel uncomfortable with, rather than repressing them; of co-operating with the new ways of being that are trying to unfold in us as long as we live, and allowing ourselves to change . . . All very healthy from the standpoint of mental hygiene, especially at potential crisis points like adolescence, mid-life and retirement, when your subpersonalities may be as confused as your Ego and need to be taken seriously to get re-orientated and to adapt to new roles. But also an ideal to aim at throughout our lives, if we are to feel authentic, fulfilled, real , and continue to grow, to be un-neurotic. For Jung, a neurosis was the penalty we paid for not being true to our selves. Neurosis, or worse, happens when we do not listen to our selves, or do not want to listen.

Our heavyweights, as we have said, the 'fat' selves, are the ones we listen to most, identify with, allow expression most often. The fattest subpersonality in anyone is the most characteristic quality of that person. Think, for example, of somebody you know well. How would you describe him or her to somebody who did not know them? After describing their physical characteristics and being met with the question: 'What is he (or she) really like as a *person*?', you would then have to pick out the quality of energy that person carries most obviously, in other words, the subpersonality they are most identified with and present themselves as in the world. So you might reply with something like: 'Oh, he (she) is a charming person, warm and friendly,' or: 'A lot of fun to be with' perhaps, if they are strong on the Pleaser or the Playful Child. On the other hand, if either of these subpersonalities is not so well developed in them as to be their salient characteristic, you might have described the person in terms of how capable or caring they were, in other words, as having a strong Good Parent subpersonality.

But although the 'fat' subpersonalities may be the stars holding centre stage, the 'thin' subpersonalities are there somewhere in the wings, waiting like understudies to make their entrance whenever they get the chance, wanting their share of the limelight. These are the subpersonalities whose growth has been stunted by our over-patronage of the 'fat' parts — which benefited from so much positive encouragement in the past from those who brought us up or from being validated by the society in which we live, the job we do, or the people whose opinion of us we value. Different qualities will be valued in different cultures: Parent qualities like seriousness, responsibility, consistency will be rewarded in 'straight' or bourgeois milieux, for example, but derided among punks or Hell's Angels. The development of such qualities may be stunted in their growth by insufficient encouragement, but always be present, at least potentially. Much of the work of probation officers, social workers and the like is precisely to foster the growth of more creative and law-abiding energies and to discourage the acting out of those that have got their clients into trouble in the past.

This is not to suggest that any subpersonality is in itself anti-social, negative or destructive. For convenience we are referring to these parts of us as if they were people, but in fact they are psychic *energies*, more or less consistently constellated complexes in the Unconscious that influence us in very specific ways whenever they become activated. Energy by itself is neutral — neither constructive nor destructive. It all depends on how it is channelled into the world. Petrol can drive a car or be used in a bomb; gas can be switched on to cook the spaghetti or to commit suicide. It is the Ego Decision-Maker that is the energy-channeller, and energy carried by a subpersonality that is clever and unconventional (as many criminals are) could be channelled into many widely different activities, from starting up a successful business, to the equally lucrative but somewhat more risky robbing a bank. It depends which other subpersonalities are adding their weight to propelling the Ego in a certain direction. In the case of the bank robber, there might well be an Adventurer subpersonality at work who thrives on the risk involved, and would have been bored stiff running a factory. In yet another person this grouping of the clever, the unconventional and the adventurous qualities could lead to a totally different career — as a drag queen, for example. The point is that being clever, unconventional or adventurous can work for you or against you — *you* decide.

Your particular ways of channelling these energies, of experiencing them and expressing them makes you the individual that you are and gives you your unique way of being in the world. This is what we mean when we say someone 'has different sides' to them, or that they 'have a lot of personality'. It is what 'makes them tick', or a 'character'. The particular ways in which these energies constellated in you were the result of both your heredity and your conditioning. You are stuck with them for the rest of your life, for energy cannot be destroyed. And you do not have to destroy them for, as we have said, each of them has a purpose in your life. In their different ways (however it may seem at the time) they are all serving you in some way, helping to keep you alive or offering the potential for further growth. Without any one of them, you would be less complete and your life would be impoverished. And so would this world, for your particular song has never been sung before on this planet quite the way you sing it.

In describing subpersonalities in the pages that follow we use the phrase 'negative aspect' in the context of whether the energy carried by each subpersonality is overdeveloped or underdeveloped, is balanced by other subpersonalities, and whether it is being channelled appropriately by the Ego. 'Appropriately' means with awareness of other subpersonalities and their needs and of the objective realities and demands of the outer world. Ignoring either or trampling on both, a subpersonality which is too fat could land you in trouble.

Let us now look at some of the subpersonalities we all have. Remember that in describing each of these subpersonalities we are trying to pin down the quality of the energy it carries. To help capture the particular 'flavour' of a subpersonality and render it less elusive, I have suggested external 'models' (rather in the style of astrologers) that appear to me to embody a certain type of energy. It may not seem that way to you and you are of course perfectly entitled to disagree and to substitute one that for you appears to be more exact. Remember, too, that the human psyche, like the universe itself and other closed energy systems, is self-regulating. This means that for every energy that exists in a person, there must be another energy that is exactly its opposite to balance it. In other words, all of us are potentially *anything*. The mild-mannered man who one day goes berserk, the pillar of society who is caught shop-lifting, the crook turned war hero, the 'tart with a heart' — these are just a few examples of a 'thin' or disowned energy managing at last to make itself heard.

THE INNER CHILD

Our Inner Child is the most important of all our subpersonalities. We were born with it and it remains with us for the rest of our lives. It never grows up. That is fortunate for otherwise we would lose our most authentic part. It is the part of us which is always young and fresh, sensitive to truth, capable of intimacy, warmth, spontaneity and love. It is our capacity to be playful, to go on learning, to be surprised and to experience a sense of wonder. It is also terribly vulnerable and easily hurt.

If your Inner Child is pulling your strings right now you could be

- feeling open, playful or loving
- a lot of fun to be with
- sulking
- singing or dancing
- playing truant from work
- throwing a tantrum
- enjoying a game such as cards or tennis
- getting ready for a fancy dress party
- feeling sad
- feeling defiant or rebellious
- feeling special
- wanting approval
- having a good time
- feeling very relaxed and happy
- very much in touch with what the people you are with are feeling

- feeling unsure and vulnerable
- feeling over-sensitive and easily hurt
- wanting attention
- lonely
- worrying about the future
- feeling timid or shy
- feeling anxious or vulnerable for no apparent reason
- suffering from agoraphobia
- feeling sorry for yourself
- feeling stressed, that things are getting on top of you
- hankering after something, not knowing what it could be
- unconsciously making yourself ill to experience the support you need.

THE VULNERABLE CHILD

The soft centre in all of us, our most intimate and sensitive core. This is the part of us that is open and capable of feeling deeply, that senses straight away whether we are with people who love and accept us or not.

This sensitivity and ability to *feel* is what makes us able to tolerate and sustain intimacy, to be *moved* by anything, music, beauty, a sunset, kindnesses shown to us by others — and other people's pain. For the Vulnerable Child inside us knows only too well what it feels like to be hurt by others' insensitivity, neglect, coldness or sheer ill will. It is only happy in an atmosphere of warmth and acceptance, knowing its fears are heard and its feelings understood, feeling safe, *held*. It is so innocent that it has not learned the ways of the world, often feels lost or confused, afraid of being punished by being abandoned by those it loves; so young that it often cannot articulate clearly what it is it needs, though it feels it.

This Child does not know how to protect itself or how to set boundaries, for it is too young. It would not know how to, just as it is not always sure exactly what it needs, only that it needs something. If your Ego is not sufficiently aware of or sympathetic to your Inner Child to protect it against getting traumatized or terrorized in the rough-and-tumble of everyday life, it becomes heavily reliant on other subpersonalities to do the job for it. Most often, in the course of therapy, a frightened Child is found hiding behind the formidable defences erected to protect it by the over-developed Controllers, Pushers and Pleasers that are causing trouble for the Ego in work and relationships and cause it to seek counselling. If these defences are penetrated too fast and without love, our Vulnerable Child, unable to tolerate such dangerous exposure to a cold and unfeeling world, might well take refuge in breakdown or illness.

Your Inner Child cannot survive long without love, for it is the subpersonality closest to your heart, your essence, your innermost being. Many of the sayings of Jesus were addressed to this part of us. And any religion that forgets to address it soon becomes dry, sterile, worldly — and loses its appeal.

Vulnerable Children at large today
Everybody has a vulnerable child inside them, usually hiding behind other subpersonalities.

Work Vulnerable Children are drawn to
None. They are too young to work. The only thing they do is *feel*.

THE HURT CHILD/ OMNIPOTENT CHILD

The negative aspect of the Vulnerable Child is the Hurt Child or the Omnipotent Child. As we shall be seeing in later chapters, any subpersonality that does not feel seen, acknowledged or accepted turns sour, for its needs are not being met. If the Vulnerable Child is hurt too often and gives up ever hoping to be loved, understood and nourished, it becomes the Hurt Child.

Hurt Children can become depressed, withdrawn or

negative; become cynical, resort to lying, avoid intimacy; bear grudges, show socially maladaptive behaviour. Since they feel nobody cares for them they become incapable of caring for other people and cultivate insensitivity — which is tantamount to deadening the Vulnerable Child that has brought them only pain. Turning their backs on the possibility of love, people whose Vulnerable Child has been very hurt by others may well develop destructive or self-destructive subpersonalities, or court power over others.

However one prefers to explain the phenomenon of a compulsive need to be special (for example in Kleinian or Adlerian terms), there appears to be a definite connection between omnipotence and vulnerability. Many famous or notorious historical figures had appalling things happen to them in childhood and perhaps it is not too fanciful to trace some connection between the traumas they underwent at the hands of their parents, with the policies they later pursued when brought to power. Good Queen Bess, for example.

Elizabeth I's tortuous diplomacy, her fear of any sort of commitment, whether to a matrimonial or political alliance, is partly explainable in terms of her mother's terrible fate that May day on Tower Green. The message this Tudor Child got loud and clear before her third birthday seems to have been 'Marriage is no fun — it can kill you', a message reinforced no doubt by her experience of four more royal stepmothers. Perhaps it was this part of the Virgin Queen that resonated so much with her own reluctant execution of her cousin Mary, Queen of Scots — another Hurt Child? — that Elizabeth nearly had a nervous breakdown.

The cynicism, aggressiveness and seedy bachelorhood of Frederick the Great are similarly understandable in terms of the subpersonalities sprouting on the wasteland created by early experience of lack of love and emotional security. One remembers the harshness with which he was treated in his youth by his father Frederick William I, King of Prussia. Not only was the feeling part of him that loved poetry and music totally invalidated by this martinet of a father who was obsessed with playing with soldiers, but it was traumatized by being forced to witness the execution of his best friend and confidante. Perhaps the message this time received loud and clear by Frederick's Vulnerable Child was: 'If you can't beat 'em join 'em' — and join in he did in the Power Game that was to plunge Europe into a succession of wars and lead to the virtual disappearance of Poland as a nation.

Once we start thinking in these terms, other examples spring to mind. How far was Napoleon affected by his foreign origin and accent, diminutive size and the pillorying these earned him at the hands of other cadets at the military school of Brienne where he was educated? His Vulnerable Child almost certainly must have experienced a lot of loneliness, wanting to run back to Mamma Letizia and his brothers and sisters in Corsica at some time or another. And, once again, we see the pattern of failure to achieve real intimacy in a love relationship: one never feels he was really *married* to either Josephine or Marie-Louise of Austria. One imagines Napoleon's Hurt Child as he leaves behind the Europe he dominated for so long aboard the *Bellerophon* escorted by his bitterest rivals, the English, and in his querulous exchanges with his jailer on St Helena. That loneliness and disappointment gnawed away at his vitals is suggested by the stomach cancer that eventually killed him.

When the Vulnerable Child's need for love is not met, and the loving energy it can generate is denied, the way is left open for more power-orientated energies to take over, and for compulsive conquest, hatred and destruction to enter the world. Energy has to go somewhere, and if it cannot flow into love it is likely to manifest as an obsession with power and the uncaring use of it.

Alice Miller has given us some clues to the genesis of Hitler's schizoid personality, to the seeds sown in his childhood that were to bear such horrific and monstrous fruit later. The brutal father who beat him almost every day, the inadequate mother incapable of defending him, let alone holding him, the part-Jewish grandfather who provides us with a clue to the later horrors.

The possible existence of a Hurt Child/Omnipotent Child in Hitler too in no way absolves him from responsibility for his crimes against humanity. We all have many sub-personalities within us (and the Hurt Child is only one sub-personality) influencing us, sometimes compulsively in certain directions. But Ego Decision-Makers cannot abdicate their responsibility for their actions while under its influences for others will be affected by those actions, sometimes millions of others.

We should now (with some relief, perhaps) look at

THE PLAYFUL CHILD

The nature of children is to play — and this is the part of you that can do things just for fun. Whenever you are enjoying yourself, it is *this* one of your many selves that is experiencing joy. It is a very valuable part of you: without it you would get even more stressed than you do, for you would never have the capacity to relax. It does not expect to take responsibility or any notice of time or obligations — and certainly not to work: these duties are for adults, not for children. The Playful Child gets totally absorbed in its games and hates to be dragged away from them for dreary things like school or cleaning up its room (or the adult equivalent, getting up for work and doing the chores). It has its favourite toys of any kind, and gets very attached to them. It is very gregarious and feels lonely without playmates, but it quickly loses interest in playing if, for any reason, it feels unsafe or gets hurt, when it disappears to make way for the Vulnerable Child. And, until the Vulnerable Child is reassured, its twin, Playful Child, will not come out to play.

Models for the Playful Child

- Danny Kaye
- Bette Midler
- Alf (in the TV series)
- Goldie Hawn
- Spike Milligan.

Activities your Playful Child might engage you in

- travel
- camping
- sport
- spending hours playing with your 'toys' such as your car or computer
- taking days off from work
- window shopping
- singing
- dancing
- playing an instrument
- playing anything
- fancy dress or fancy dressing
- telling jokes or playing practical ones.

Unless you allow this part of you to come out and be non-serious from time to time, your life will be joyless. You will tend to take things too seriously, find it hard to relax and enjoy yourself, be pessimistic and get easily stressed. When things are really going badly this subpersonality can be a life-saver by getting you to see the funny side. People will appreciate this quality in you, for it helps them to lighten up too. There is a time to be serious and to work — and playtime, a time to ease up, take a break, and enjoy the fruits of your labour. The times spent 'playing' (whatever that means for you) are precious: we talk about 'having a good time' and 'the time of our lives'. Understandably, for when your Child is playing (for example, when you are enjoying a good holiday) you feel you are really living. You may murmur blissfully to your companion on the adjacent mattress as you thirstily soak up the sun and sip an iced something. 'This is what Life is all about!'

NEGATIVE ASPECTS OF THE PLAYFUL CHILD

All subpersonalities, however, even Playful Child, have their negative possibilities, depending on how we relate to them, whether or not they are sufficiently balanced by other subpersonalities, and the awareness or appropriateness with which they are allowed to come out. It is the responsibility of the Ego to decide whether the expression of the energy carried by a subpersonality is going to be positive or destructive, either for oneself or for other people.

The negative aspects of the Playful Child are precisely those we might expect of children who get carried away by the game and go 'over the top'. They take the game too seriously, fight over the most trivial points of procedure, invent scary initiation rituals, cannot bear to lose. William Golding's novel *Lord of the Flies*, described how cruel children can be to those who cannot play the game as well as they can, and bully those weaker than themselves. The Playful Child never knows when to stop, when the game has gone far enough and Omnipotent Child is beginning to take over.

If your Playful Child goes 'over the top' it could make you

- go on any sort of binge
- get into a brawl
- a bully
- run up gambling debts
- be irresponsible and unreliable
- be a bad loser
- be a football hooligan
- be in trouble with the law
- be a pain in the neck if nobody else is into their own Playful Child.

THE MAGICAL CHILD

Magical Child loves the world of make-believe, dressing up and playing 'let's pretend'. It is immensely curious, original and creative. It is the imaginative part of you, the romantic and the dreamer of dreams. It enjoys stories with heroes and heroines, witches and warlocks, of lost worlds and far-flung planets. It has a special relationship with Nature and the animal world and never loses its sense of wonder and awe. When highly developed, it gives you an intuitive understanding of the Eternal Truths at the heart of all religion, and any religion that ceases to address this Child loses its soul.

Models for the Magical Child

- The Little Prince
- Snow White
- Alice in Wonderland
- Peter Pan
- ET.

Your Magical Child could influence you to become

- a magician, conjuror or ventriloquist
- an actor or actress
- anything to do with the theatre
- a theatre-goer
- fascinated with the esoteric or the occult
- an astrologer, fortune-teller or tarot reader
- a lover of nature
- a novelist
- an artist or sculptor
- an avid reader of science fiction
- a fashion designer or model
- a scientist
- a seeker after enlightenment
- the disciple of a guru.

Creative people with a highly developed Magical Child

- Shakespeare
- Mozart
- Hans Christian Andersen
- Albert Einstein
- Charlie Chaplin
- Sir Laurence Olivier
- Steven Spielberg
- Coco the Clown
- The Beatles
- Yves St Laurent
- Boy George.

NEGATIVE ASPECTS OF THE MAGICAL CHILD

If the Magical Child is not balanced by an earthier sub-personality it could become so caught up in its fantasies that it loses touch with what is real and what is not. An example of this is Blanche in the Tennessee Williams' play *A Streetcar named Desire*. Her *cri de coeur* 'Who wants reality? I want *magic*' is the key to her deterioration and final breakdown. Blinded by her Vulnerable Child, her Magical Child was unable to *see* the magic of ordinary life and therefore had to try to *impose* it. In so doing she got the worst of both worlds. She offended the people around her by her airs and graces and was in turn wounded deeply by their lack of grace towards her and their refusal to accept her (until the very end) on her own terms. Her magical way of seeing the world was in fact a defence of her Vulnerable Child, whose needs could not be acknowledged without dropping her illusions about herself. These illusions were brutally shattered by a man, Stanley, who felt challenged to bring her down to earth because she invalidated the earthier energies he embodied. Finally, Blanche's Vulnerable Child was left so painfully exposed that she retreated into madness.

The Magical Child is so seductive that it can lead us too far away from this earth, make us lose touch with or turn our backs on basic and sometimes harsh realities, look down on 'ordinary' people who do not share its enthusiasms as 'dull' or 'unaware'. They, in turn, will be suspicious of our attempts to 'turn them on' and judge us mad or at least cranky. The Magical Child can get so hooked on far-out experiences that it does not see (or does not care) that its kid brother, the Vulnerable Child, is wilting away from lack of nourishment and care. The Magical Child needs always to be balanced by some more grounded subpersonality, for example the Parent, if it is not to lead us astray.

If you allow your Magical Child to pull your strings you could

- become a fanatic
- become a drug abuser
- be conned by a false guru
- give your money away to a sect
- dabble in black magic
- lose touch with what's real and what isn't
- dream your life away
- bore your friends to death.

THE INNER PARENT

The Parent is the subpersonality that developed to protect our vulnerability. It was formed out of our early experiences of the way we were treated by parents, teachers and other significant adults, and their expectations of us. The function of our Inner Parent is to look after the Inner Child. Whether our Child feels secure out in the world and is able to play and to learn or not depends on how well it is doing its job.

The Inner Parent has two aspects: nurturing, and protecting/controlling.

If your Inner Parent is balanced you will be

- able to take care of yourself
- good at taking responsibility
- able to take charge
- capable of setting boundaries
- concerned with others' well being
- a sympathetic listener
- reliable
- supportive
- a nourishing person to be with
- a good friend
- strong in time of crisis or emergency
- socially aware

You will make a good

- parent
- cook
- teacher
- manager
- social worker
- counsellor
- doctor
- nurse
- policeman or woman
- army officer
- political leader
- priest

If your Inner Parent is pulling your strings you could be

- very controlling
- over-protective
- manipulative
- bossy
- fussy
- uptight
- dogmatic
- a martyr
- drained
- judgemental
- ultra-conservative
- taking on more responsibility than you should

THE NURTURING PARENT

This is the part of you that is responsible, caring and able to give. If you are fortunate enough to have a well-developed and balanced Nurturing Parent you will be your own best friend in bad times, and also care about others. Your Nurturing Parent will make sure you look after your health, eat regular meals, get enough exercise, enough sleep. It will enable you to survive even a bed-sitter existence. Whenever you are feeling down, it will jolly you out of your depression by getting you to invite friends round or to distract yourself by getting immersed in a good book or going out to a movie. It wants the best for you and makes you feel that you deserve the good things of life.

This part of you will ensure that you never lack for friends, for it makes people relax and feel safe with you. They will enjoy the way you nourish them, whether at the dinner parties at which you are such a charming and attractive host, or with good advice when they are down. The Nurturing Parent makes you a good listener, sympathetic and supportive. It *cares* for people, and wants them to be happy. It is particularly good at handling the Vulnerable Child in others, at calming and reassuring, at holding and soothing their Hurt Child. They will come to you for advice about their problems, or feel they can unburden themselves with you, for they sense that you understand and wish them well. The Nurturing Parent is the *goodness* in you, and the stuff of which saints are made.

Models of the Inner Nurturing Parent

- Saint Francis of Assisi
- Albert Schweitzer
- Mother Teresa
- the Pope.

Your Nurturing Parent will influence you to vote

- for the Party you think *cares* most
- for the candidate who looks the *nicest*.

NEGATIVE ASPECTS OF THE NURTURING PARENT

If your Nurturing Parent is over-developed or unbalanced it could cause problems for you. This subpersonality can be a little manic and obsessive if it gets out of control. The 'Jewish Mother' syndrome is an archetypal example of the Nurturing Parent that wants to feed us, but is insensitive to whether we are in fact hungry or not, or whether we would prefer to try something other than what is on offer. They do it with love, but without awareness of where the loved one they want to nourish is 'at'. So what they get back is interpreted as rejection of their love — which in turn leads to the Martyr Syndrome expressed in recriminations like: 'You never appreciate *anything* I try to do for you' or: 'I don't know why I bother, when all I get is ' — or the even more manipulative: 'You'll miss me when I'm gone!'

The Nurturing Parents' zeal to nourish the world, if not balanced by another subpersonality, can make them end up not only as martyrs, but also totally drained and exhausted. They get so hooked into nourishing the Vulnerable Child in others that they forget to nourish their own Inner Child. This is something that anybody who works in a helping capacity with other people has to be careful to watch, John for example.

WHO NOURISHES THE NOURISHER?

John is a perfect example of somebody whose strings are being pulled by his inner Nurturing Parent to such an extent that he is dangerously near making himself ill. This in fact is a potential hazard when any subpersonality is allowed to monopolize our energies so that we get obsessed with and depleted by its demands upon us.

John is a social worker and a very dedicated and effective one. He is also a typical example of a 'wounded healer' — somebody drawn to working in a helping profession and supporting the Hurt Child in others as an indirect way of relieving the anxiety and insecurity of his own Inner Child. This subpersonality in him recognizes and resonates with (is activated by) the insecurity and desperation he sees in his clients. Such empathy is what makes him good at his job, for his clients sense that he is on their side, feel seen and heard by him, trust him. But John's unawareness that he is identified with his Nurturing Parent (and why) means that he cannot switch off its energy when he needs to — and allow himself to relax and be nourished in turn for an change.

How this manifests in his life is that he works longer hours than he needs to or should, brings work home with him at night, worries about his cases when off-duty, feels totally responsible for them. And he is getting more and more exhausted, drained and irritable. He has recently been involved in conflict with his team and his supervisor over what he considers to be their hard line with one of his clients whom he considers to be particularly at risk.

They, on the other hand, are getting irritated with John for making a heavy job even heavier by being over-zealous, over-serious and over-involved with his cases. Which makes his Vulnerable Child feel even more unsupported — which makes his Parent work even harder. If John continues to allow his strings to be pulled by his Inner Parent, does not become more aware of his own motivations and the needs of his own Child, he could well be in for a breakdown of some sort.

John's Nurturing Parent provides him with the right sort of energy to do the job he does, but does not know when to stop. But then that is not its job. A Nurturing Parent's job is to *nurture* — and to go on nurturing. Each subpersonality does what it does, and only what it does. It is the job of the Ego Decision-Maker to balance the way in which the energies carried by our subpersonalities get expressed in our lives: how, how much and when. For our Ego, unlike our subpersonalities, it is the only part of us that is able (ideally) to see the whole picture and be in touch with both inner pressures to act and the objective demands of the outer world. In other words, it is the job, not of subpersonalities, but our 'I' to keep an eye on what is appropriate behaviour and what is not. John's heart is in the right place, but not his awareness.

THE PROTECTOR

This is another aspect of your Parent subpersonality and a sort of built-in guide to survival. It is the one that makes you look automatically both ways before crossing a busy street, button up your coat before going out into the cold, remember to dry your hair properly . . . Sounds familiar? Yes, it is the internalized voice of Mummy and Daddy who were always watchful to see that you did not fall ill, get hurt or expose yourself to danger. Without this subpersonality to protect you and make you more aware of the hazards of life, you might not be here now, for you might have been run over by a bus or otherwise caught your death.

Like your real parents, the Protector subpersonality warns, watches, acts to safeguard you from damaging yourself through unawareness of danger, or getting damaged by others . . . Premonitions, dreams, intuitions that something is not quite right — these are messages from this part of you whose primary function is to ensure that you survive, at all costs. The more you heed its voice, the more finely-tuned you become to potentially dangerous situations and vibrations. For example it can tell you whom you can trust and whom you would be better advised not to, or when to turn down an offer because of the hassles it may involve you in. By 'inner voice' I mean a subtle shrinking inside, a sort of sinking feeling as opposed to warm and positive spontaneous response, a feeling of lightness or even a rush of energy and enthusiasm. What we call 'hunches' or a 'sixth sense' originate for the most part from this subpersonality. The well-documented examples of people who have avoided catastrophe by, say, cancelling an air flight or selling shares before a crash were no doubt heeding messages from their Inner Protector in the subconscious.

If, however, the Protector cannot restrain us from a self-destructive course by whispered warnings, it may have to resort to shouting. A nightmare is your subconscious shouting loud, if not necessarily clear, for the message in dreams, as we shall see, are coded ones. It may have to physically restrain you from dangerously draining yourself by overwork, by making you take to your bed, with a cold, for example, or something more serious. Indeed, from a holistic viewpoint, all symptoms of acute illness are the outer signs of the struggle going on inside the body to prevent even worse 'dis-ease' and possibly death. Your Protector has the biggest arsenal of weapons at its disposal than any other subpersonality — and rightly so, for its job is primary — to keep you alive and to stop you going mad. What a psychotherapist would call a person's 'defences', such as denial, withdrawal, projection, are the Protector's way of keeping them sane. To be neurotic, however uncomfortable, is better than becoming psychotic and falling apart.

Models of the Protecting Parent

- Your 'guardian angel'
- Churches
- the medical profession
- the nursing profession
- insurance
- United Nations
- World Health Organization

THE CONTROLLER

Another aspect of the Parent subpersonality — and one you should be grateful for, for it has succeeded (we hope) in keeping you out of jail. The Controller is the sum total of all the 'dos' and 'don'ts' you have assimilated over the years — rules which keep you out of trouble with parents, teachers, the police, plus any religious upbringing you may have had. To this introjected (internalized) equivalent of the Ten Commandments plus Constance Spry you added your own accumulated experience of how to move in the society in which you live without giving yourself a hard time.

It is the part of us that knows 'how to behave' and 'do the right thing'. Without this part of us it would be hard for us to 'fit in' and be accepted in most conventional milieux. Indeed, unless an adequate Controller had been developed in us it would be hard for us to live in any form of society, for there would be no subpersonality sufficiently strong to check and monitor our instinctual energies of aggressiveness and sex, which might then be acted out freely. A balanced Controller will (in conjunction with our Critic) have a sense of what is right, acceptable and appropriate, and filter out these primal energies. If it stopped functioning, society might have to do our controlling for us — under lock and key — to protect others. Of all our subpersonalities therefore, our Controller is the one that most carries the energy of Freud's Superego. It approximates to most people's idea of a conscience, and keeps a tight rein on the expression of your 'id'. If our id does slip out and behaves rather badly (as it can for example, when the Controller has been numbed by alcohol or other drugs), we are likely to experience a backlash from the Superego in the form of guilt or fear of punishment (as well as a hangover).

The Controller has a protecting function, just as controlling is part of the repertoire of the Protector. They carry much the same sort of energy, for their function is basically the same — to ward off danger and to keep us functioning in the world. They work so closely together that the distinction between them is often blurred: they join forces whenever they feel we are threatened and aid and abet each other. We shall therefore henceforth refer to these two energies jointly as the Protector-Controller. The voice of this subpersonality can be very strident, especially if it is threatened or challenged.

Outer models of the Inner Protecting-Controlling Parent

- Moses
- Mrs Thatcher

Your Protector-Controller will influence you to vote for

- the 'strongest' candidate
- the party that promises to maintain law, order, property and traditional values

NEGATIVE ASPECT OF THE PROTECTOR-CONTROLLER

The negative aspect of the Protecting-Controlling Parent subpersonality is that, like a real parent, it can be overprotective or too repressive.

If we have imbibed the view from our real parents that the world is a very dangerous place indeed, if we were warned to be careful every time we started to touch or explore anything, to take care lest we fall, break something or cut ourselves, we may have developed a Protector-Controller that is over-vigilant and over-anxious, and for which 'safety first' has become a way of life. Like a horse that is too highly strung, it tenses up in unfamiliar situations, shies away from new challenges life puts before it, balks at the molehills that in its panic it perceives as mountains. It makes us too suspicious for intimacy, withdrawing nervously from anyone who tries to get too close, ignoring or refusing any goodies they hold out to us because we fear they may be trying to trap us in some way. A paranoid Protector-Controller stops us taking any sort of risk, rules out adventure, keeps us trapped in the safe, the known and familiar, in a rut.

It is the subpersonality that is most likely to be pulling your strings when you start feeling ill at ease in a situation, for it is warning you to withdraw from what it perceives as a threat. If for some reason, professional or social, it is not at that moment possible or appropriate for you to withdraw, your Protector-Controller may well give you something like stage-fright, agoraphobia or claustrophobia, or sabotage your performance by making you freeze or clam up. It needs the strongest defensive weapons at its disposal, for it is the part of you that is entrusted with your survival. And, if necessary, to protect you from your self (or rather, from your other selves that might lead you astray). If all else fails, it could make you ill to get you home safely to bed, or threaten to if you don't watch out and take better care (which is what makes us hypochondriacs). It is also very clever at staging 'accidents' at the times most inconvenient for other subpersonalities that want you to have fun and let your hair down, or which have persuaded you to embark on something challenging, exciting or faintly risky. But then, when your Protector-Controller takes over, the other subpersonalities don't stand a chance. It is the Heavyweight of them all.

The negative aspect of the Protector-Controller is experienced by the Ego as inhibition, paranoia and guilt, and by others as authoritarianism, repressiveness and joylessness. It is the authority figure that punishes us in our own best interests — the cartoon headmaster brandishing the cane with the words: 'This is going to hurt me more than it hurts you, my boy' ballooning out of his mouth.

To have to remain so constantly on the alert for possible threats to our safety makes one tense. If your Protector is working overtime you will tend to be a pessimist. You will also tend to over-react, and much of what you do will be concerned with taking steps to forestall the materialization of your catastrophic expectations. But whatever you do, this subpersonality will never allow you to feel that you have done enough to make the Vulnerable Child feel truly safe. And the more vulnerable your Child, the more obsessive your Protector-Controller feels it has to be. It will therefore enlist the aid of the other subpersonalities, such as the Pleaser and the Pusher, to erect a string of defences around the child to ensure it does not get hurt.

The Protector-Controller is the self that many people identify with most and get most uptight about if it is challenged or invalidated in any way. The more vulnerable their Inner Child is, the less it has felt held in the past, the more rigid, uncompromising and watchful their Protector-Controller has to be to relieve its paranoia.

This type of Protector-Controller assumes that the way it has learned to see the world is 'common sense' and anybody who disagrees with its views must therefore be either dishonest or mad. It can therefore make us extremely dogmatic and closed to new ideas. And, if these new ideas are considered too dangerous to its values the Protector-Controller may consider itself justified in stamping them out to maintain its own authority. So fearful is it of anarchy or subversion that it may resort to *any* means to secure the status quo.

The energy carried by this subpersonality is manifested in the world today by absolutist governments and their secret police and intelligence organizations backed up by the military. The essential quality of this subpersonality is *repression* of anything considered dangerous, and this applies as much to the inner as to the outer world. If your Protector-Controller is pulling your strings (as well as trying to protect you), it will have a strangle hold on what you allow yourself to think, feel and do. Spontaneous you certainly will not be, nor joyful. More like uptight and conventional, controlled and controlling, for your Playful Child will be being kept under a tight rein in case it gets hurt or out of hand. For the Negative Protector-Controller *all* Playful Children are hippies, punks or hooligans.

Favourite expressions of the negative Protector-Controller

- 'It shouldn't be allowed'
- 'Bring back the birch, capital punishment' (anything that's painful)
- 'Sexual offenders should be castrated'
- 'What's this country coming to?'
- 'We must defend ourselves, whatever the cost'.

Favourite pastimes of very negative Protector-Controllers

- apartheid
- Ku-Klux-Klan
- working for the CIA
- witch-hunts
- queer-bashing
- Paki-bashing
- bashing anyone seen as a threat.

MEET THE BOSS
Your back-seat driver

The Driver is the most up front of all your subpersonalities. This is the part of you that is continually pushing you to do things, to get on, to get on with it, to get somewhere. Its voice is one of the clearest and most familiar of any of your selves. To hear it, just sit down intending to relax and listen to it telling you all the reasons why you simply don't have time to relax. There are too many chores that have to be done. It will remind you of the jobs around the house that you have been putting off, the letters you have to write, the phone calls you have to make. It will make you hurry when there is no need, run for the bus, and if you miss it, wait, fuming or fretting, scanning the horizon for the next one. It will feed you ideas about how to further your projects and ambitions and fire you with the necessary enthusiasms and energy. It hovers around like an over-conscientious secretary, diary at the ready, inside your head, setting up new appointments and commitments for you as soon as it sees you have a moment to yourself. As soon as one job or project is complete (or even before) it lines up new ones for you, for it cannot bear unstructured time. Your driver is, quite simply, the pressure you put on yourself, and is often (as in the case of workaholics) a Slave Driver. It is a staunch ally of your Protector-Controller and your Critic, and works together with them to make sure you toe the line, come up to scratch, put in a good performance, and don't let the side down.

If your Driver has been pulling your strings you could be

- ambitious
- successful
- very busy
- self-assertive
- a demanding employer
- working overtime
- promoted
- well-off
- super-efficient
- a workaholic
- never with a free moment
- on the verge of a nervous breakdown
- suffering from a stomach ulcer
- a candidate for a coronary
- unable to unwind
- insomniac
- exhausted
- divorced.

Like the Protector-Controller, the Driver's survival function is to protect your Vulnerable Child against destitution, being ignored or being punished for not doing what it is supposed to be doing. It is really the internalized voices of the teachers who used to write on your school reports 'Must work harder if he is to succeed'. And this is what your Driver wants for you, to work harder so that you achieve the experience of success at something, feel you are somebody, are on top of things, get ahead – or at least, don't get left behind. Without your Driver you would never be able to get anything together.

A balanced Driver should ensure that you do well, make money, hold down a job, get promoted. It makes you a good worker, well motivated, energetic, with the drive necessary to initiate new projects and carry them through. It will ensure that you get up in the mornings even after a late night out, are into the office on time, stay on top of your job, are approved of by the boss – and eventually become the boss. There are some jobs that you would not have the right energy for unless your Driver was well-developed. And, however great the talent you were born with, without the discipline necessary to develop and refine it, you are unlikely to reach the top. Or to be a genius, defined by our friend Frederick the Great as having 'an infinite capacity for taking pains'.

Jobs needing strong Drivers

- politicians (especially Prime Ministers)
- salesmen and saleswomen
- sergeant-majors
- explorers
- reformers
- executives
- investigators
- reporters
- organizers
- publicity agents
- property developers.

Models of the Internal Driver

- the 'back-seat driver'
- army NCOs
- naval Petty Officers
- cheer-leaders
- sports coaches
- Winston Churchill (during the Second World War)
- Lady Macbeth.

THE OVERDEVELOPED DRIVER

The more anxious you are about making it (perhaps through experience of early deprivation or a particularly virulent Inferiority Complex), the more pushy this Pusher inside you is likely to be – and to turn people off. The foot-in-the-door salesman desperate to sell at least one brush, vacuum cleaner or encyclopaedia before giving up for the day can be quite threatening; the 'hard sell' of the commission-hungry makes potential customers feel pressurized and antagonistic; the publicity-seeking of the would-be-famous arouse our scorn. And, even if you do make it through your determination, hard work and talent, there is always the possibility that others might envy you. Unlike the Pleaser, the Driver is more intent on good performance than harmonious relationships, and, if others stand in the way of its ambitions and driving energy, it can be quite ruthless.

More serious, though, are the possible effects of too much work and no play on your own well-being and relationships. Couples who spend the day working together are particularly at risk from the havoc the competitiveness of their Drivers can wreak when they get home at night.

The Driver may well be trying to protect the Vulnerable Child in you, but, in the process of trying to make this little one feel safe by being adequately provided for, it tends often to lock up the Playful Child, not even allowing it out to play every so often. There just isn't any *time* for any activities which do not in some way further the ambitious or implement the programme of the Driver, for this part of you is totally goal-orientated. In order to keep you from feeling the strain of burning the midnight oil too often, to help you to allow yourself space during the day to relax, to make sure you don't miss your lunch breaks, there needs to be a strong Nourishing Parent around in you. It will tell you when enough is enough and it is time to go to bed. The Driver is the subpersonality most likely to make you ill and fall victim to some form of stress disease. And, if you don't allow time for recreation, for enjoying the fruits of your labour, then the quality of your life, as well as your health could be impoverished. You won't see enough of the people you love, or, if you do, they might become bored with hearing only about your work. And, if they give up on you and start looking elsewhere for playmates, your Vulnerable Child will feel deprived and abandoned.

HARRY, CANDIDATE FOR A CORONARY

You will remember Harry if you read my book *How to Beat Fatigue* as somebody who desperately needed to learn how to relax and take it easy. Harry made it from East End barrow boy to Oxford Street store owner by sheer hard work and now cannot stop. He has a manager but does not trust him to bring in the customers and the money in sufficient quantities to enable Harry and Rachel to stay at home in their mansion in one of the smarter suburbs. Or so he says. Rachel thinks this is ridiculous and tells her husband that they are well off already, and could retire any time they wanted — and that David, their store manager, is doing a great job. She knows the truth, however: her husband is so addicted to work that he just cannot let go of it. For so many years it has been his life. It has brought him wealth to provide a home for himself and his wife, to set his sons up in business, to give him sense of achievement, to earn respect in the community. Harry's whole self-image is inextricably entwined with his Driver, he is identified with it. So he cannot keep away from Oxford Street, checking the takings, discussing the buying, worrying over the competition — acting as if was still on the way up rather than, as is the case, having arrived. When his inner Driver made him start talking about opening another store Rachel put her foot down. She is frightened that he will kill himself unless he lets up. But the Driver never lets up: it is not its nature. It will make a donkey out of us and hold the carrot of 'more' in front of us until we drop. It doesn't care. For it knows that for every Harry who drops dead with a coronary, there are millions more Harries carrying the Driver's 'Type A' energy who will be only too willing to become its slaves.

THE UNDERDEVELOPED DRIVER

Models:

- layabouts
- laid-backs

In a culture like ours that values success and effective performance so highly, anyone with an underdeveloped Driver is likely to be disadvantaged in one way or another. They may well be judged as adversely as those who try to fly too high, but are more likely to be looked down upon than envied.

MARK

As a schoolboy Mark was often in trouble with teachers for not doing his homework. He would, in fact, only do it when the pressure became too strong, not only at school but also from his anxious parents. Even then he would usually either not finish it, or hand in carelessly written, untidy work. It was not that he was not bright, but that he resented having to study subjects he did not see the point of, or was not interested in. Telling him that he would see the use of them after he got his school-leaving certificates and got a job cut no ice with him. Much of his time in the classroom was spent in doing the minimum work to keep out of trouble and daydreaming about himself as a rock star (when not immersed in carving initials on the side of his desk, out of view of the teacher).

The same pattern recurred after Mark left school. He had a succession of jobs, but could stick at nothing long, for the ones he was interested in needed extra qualifications, and the ones he got did not interest him. His laziness and casual attitude towards his work got him into trouble with his employers, just as it had at school. Yielding to parental exhortation to 'go for something that interests you', he enrolled for a course in design at an art college where some of his friends were studying, thinking it would be 'fun'. Because of his unwillingness to apply himself, and his resistance to any form of guidance, he was advised by the college that there was no point in completing the course. Since then Mark has been on the dole, half-heartedly looking for jobs that he does not really want to find, beginning to think of himself as a failure and getting in with what his parents consider as 'the wrong crowd'.

Take your driving test now

- Make a list of all the things that you should have done by now but did not have time for because you were too busy.
- Add to this list the other things you would be able to do if you had more time.

How many items did your list include?

- 0 – No wonder the house is a mess and you are always broke.
- Between 1 and 5 – Your Driver sounds alive and well.
- Between 5 and 10 – Maybe you are trying to fly too high?
- Over 10 – Do I smell burning? Your Driver is overdeveloped and over the top. Seriously, ease up before you burn up.

LOVE ME DO
The pleaser

This is the part of you that is always *nice* to people and tries to keep everybody happy. Its function, like that of your Inner Parent, is to protect your Child by ensuring you are loved, and to forestall attack from others. Your Pleaser feels very uncomfortable if you are disliked or disapproved of in any way, and is very sensitive to criticism in any shape or form.

Your Pleaser started to develop very early on as a result of feedback from what pleased Mummy and what didn't: the things you did as a toddler that made her stiffen up and frown alarmingly (or even scarier, scold), or those that made her smile and beam warmth and love down on you. The most important thing in your life for years was learning how not to lose that love, that warmth. When it seemed temporarily to disappear (at a certain stage in your development, even if she left the room), you felt abandoned, desolated, and you feared it might never come back. Perhaps, in your childish fantasies of omnipotence, you overestimated the sheer power of your naughtiness. You thought that, if you sensed mother's fatigue, it was you who were draining her and might kill her. That if she got too angry with you, she might give you away . . . that, if your parents separated, it was your fault and that you were just too much trouble.

At school, a large part of what we call 'education' consisted in pleasing our teachers and keeping out of trouble. The Nemesis that inexorably followed failure to do so (at least, if we were caught out) took various forms, from the mild to the draconian, from a mere tongue-lashing, through lines, detention or suspension of privileges to a real beating. And, in fact, pleasing your teacher by doing your homework and behaving in class meant the difference between good and bad reports to take home to show your parents – and whether or not you passed your exams.

Your Pleaser is now well developed and has got the message 'pleasing pays off', in making you feel secure and in getting on in life. Unless, of course, it has tried too often and failed to achieve either, in which case it gives up trying to please at all and the energy goes into forming another subpersonality to defend the Child. (The Rebel, is one of these – more concerned, however, with protecting the Playful Child than the Vulnerable Child.) But, even if denied, deep down, the need for love and recognition remains throughout our lives.

Out in the world as a young adult one learns that the same laws apply as at school and in the home. The penalties for not meeting the expectations of the interviewer for a job, the boss (if we have pleased enough to get the job), the boy or girl friend, are dire: once again either loss of love or loss of position. By trial and error we learn more about the art of pleasing, what works and what doesn't, and form habits that work consistently when presenting ourselves, as short cuts to instant acceptance and securing the confidence of others. We learn to use the smile, the tone of voice, the gestures, the jokes: to disarm, to seduce, to win others over to our side.

Pleasers are very useful subpersonalities in getting us through life with the minimum of abrasiveness, the maximum of good vibrations from others. People will usually respond to your Pleaser's politeness, courtesy and charm in similar fashion (unless their own undeveloped Pleaser makes them boorish). If they are uptight for any reason they will feel mollified, soothed by it and, if angry with you, their anger may well be deflected. For one lesson the Pleaser has learned is that 'a soft answer turneth away wrath'. This subpersonality forms a large part of what Jung called the *persona*, the mask that, like the actors in ancient Greece, we put on to face our audience and deliver our performance. Without a strong Pleaser, some jobs would be impossible to do well, if at all.

Model of an effective Pleaser

- Ronald Reagan

Jobs that need a strong Pleaser subpersonality to do well

- public relations
- diplomatic corps
- airline steward and stewardess
- waiter and waitress
- hotel manager, receptionist, doorman
- advertising
- hostess
- shop assistant
- secretary
- butler
- maid

NEGATIVE ASPECTS OF THE PLEASER

If your pleaser is overdeveloped you could end up totally drained or a doormat — or both, if such a thing as a totally drained doormat exists anywhere at all.

Meeting other people's expectations takes a lot of patience and energy, and the more they get used to your meeting them, the more they will take this — and you — for granted. The more of their demands you meet, the more demanding they will tend to become. The Pleaser can make it very hard for you to say 'no' or to set boundaries to how far you are prepared to go to keep the other person happy. If you do, in a lapse from your usual grace, give way to irritation or impatience (God forbid you should actually get angry and say anything unkind!) your Pleaser will immediately make you feel guilty and your Vulnerable Child feel unprotected. Both fear the consequences of your outburst: either you will provoke attack, be disliked or lose your job.

Because you cannot say a firm 'no' to people (and it can be done politely if your Pleaser is balanced) you run the risk of doing more than anyone has the right to expect from you, subjecting yourself to more stress and fatigue than you need to. A particularly lethal alliance of subpersonalities is that of excessive Pleaser plus excessive Nurturing Parent. These two between them could crowd out virtually every other subpersonality and together create the Martyr whose life is sacrificed on the cross of the needs and expectations of others and whose own needs are seen as of little or no value by comparison.

And, because you cannot bring yourself to say 'no', even when other parts of you are grumbling away inside at being thus ignored, people you are trying so hard to please will not trust your 'yes' that is trotted out so automatically. They will not trust *you*, that you really mean what you say, that you will be there for them when they really need you. Also, much as your honeyed words may flatter their egos, they may sense that they will never hear the truth from you, things perhaps that, though not as palatable as honey, they nevertheless need to hear. For your Pleaser makes you report only what you think people want to hear, rather than what you really feel to be the truth. In other words, your Pleaser may well get you the reputation for at best, lightweight or superficial, at worst, phoney or untrustworthy. But at least you will have people around you. If your Pleaser is quite nonexistent, it is possible you will have none.

SAM: A DESPERATE PLEASER

Sam is an example of a person whose Pleaser is pulling his strings so relentlessly that the only way he can get relief is to desensitize himself to this subpersonality by getting drunk. This then gives him an excuse to behave badly (drop his persona, rebel) without having to take responsibility for it, for he can claim that he does not remember a thing.

We have seen that subpersonalities develop in the first place to serve us, and overdevelop whenever more of this particular energy is needed to protect us in some way. In Sam's case, developing a strong Pleaser lessened the oppressive guilt that might have made him seriously depressed. The eldest of three sons and the only one who was born without a handicap, in some way he felt that he had sapped his mother's energy so that there had not been enough left for her to produce more normal children. The family was poor and, particularly after the father died, Sam's mother had to work extra hard to make ends meet. He helped her as much as he could, working extra hours at the factory, handing over the wage packet, spending time with his handicapped brothers after work instead of going out. He never felt he could ask for anything for himself at home, for it seemed obvious that his brothers had priority. To have added to the burdens already bravely borne by his mother was unthinkable.

After his mother died the younger boys were institutionalized, for their condition had deteriorated. Sam felt bad about this, and even more so because at one level he also felt a sense of relief that he could now be freer and have a life of his own. He moved to a big city and got a job in a hospital as a porter. Predictably, his Pleaser was by now so much a part of him he would only feel comfortable working in a job where he was at everybody's beck and call. And, at the hospital, he certainly was. After a day wheeling trolleys, escorting patients up and down in lifts, being kind and encouraging to all and sundry, feeling that he was not doing enough, and responsible for their comfort, Sam would return home exhausted and drained, feeling hollow inside.

But since he lived alone and there was nobody for his Pleaser to please, the energy of this subpersonality now had no outlet. Sam did not know what to do with this self. He would bathe, try to relax, watch some television — but eventually his restlessness would take him out to the bars where he would inevitably get drunk and, more often than not, become so surly and provocative to other customers that the barman would refuse to serve him any more drink. This denial of the 'nipple' would enrage him, for it resonated with his disowned resentment at having had to 'feed' everyone else, his mother and brothers, the patients he worked with, while his Inner Child went unnourished. At this point he would often be asked to leave, and would slither off the bar-stool and lurch off with much cursing to find another outlet for his frustration. Next morning he would wake up hung over, feeling guilty, and broke, for his wages were not high enough to support these binges.

Sam's overdeveloped Pleaser (fattened by his identification with Nurturing Parent) is splitting him into two polarized parts, between which he swings as predictably as a clock pendulum. Another, less lightweight subpersonality at times has to take over from the Pleaser so that Sam can feel he exists at all, for when the Pleaser is in operation Sam disappears entirely in the sense of being in touch with any needs or desires of his own. He has never learned that sometimes, and especially in the interests of sanity, it is OK to please yourself, and necessary to allow your Inner Child out to play. But then he would not know how to do this without feeling guilty. To resolve this Superego-Id conflict, Sam's Ego has to start setting boundaries to both. Both his Pleaser and its shadow, the Bully, have to be cut down to size so that he can do a good job during the day at work, *and* relax and play without feeling guilty afterwards.

Test for whether your Pleaser is out of control and running your life. When did you last

- go ahead with something you wanted to do in spite of opposition
- refuse a request for something you did not want to give
- withdraw from an interaction that was draining you
- tell a friend what you thought about his/her self-destructive behaviour
- enjoy a mock-bitchy verbal battle just for fun

- refuse to be manipulated into doing something you did not want to do
- give yourself permission to let your hair down and be a little outrageous
- not meet an expectation
- refuse to be made to feel guilty for not meeting an expectation?

Are you able to ask

- somebody upsetting your guests to leave
- for what you need, for instance for money owed to you
- a fair price for your service or something you are selling?

When you feel irritated or angry with someone do you

- tell them and feel bad about telling them
- not tell them and wish you had
- smile or laugh
- tell them you understand how *they* must feel
- try to smooth it over
- say 'I'm sure you are right'
- freeze?

The question to ask your Pleaser is: 'Are you getting for me what *I* need, or are you selling me short?' Pleasing others rather than pleasing oneself is sometimes not in one's own best interests. OK — so everybody loves you. But does anybody respect you? And by the way, how hard did your Pleaser make you try to find the answers to these questions? Or was it your Driver?

BE YE PERFECT
Your inner critic

The Inner Critic, like the Protector-Controller, is an aspect of our Superego and comes close to what we normally refer to as our 'conscience'. It is the part of us capable of reflecting on what we do and giving us feedback. Without it, we would have no yardstick by which to assess how we are doing, no ability to discriminate between what is good and what is mediocre or rubbish. We would have neither 'taste' nor 'style'.

If your Inner Critic is pulling your strings you could be

- discriminating
- honest with yourself
- capable of grasping fine distinctions
- the best judge of your own work
- having a low opinion of yourself
- punishing yourself
- intensely critical of yourself and others
- a perfectionist
- a self-improver
- depressed
- lacking confidence
- obsessively neat and tidy
- often feeling guilty.

Model of the Inner Critic

- a judge

Your Critic, if it is backed up by the capacity for hard work of a well-developed Pusher is what most makes for genius and originality in any field, for it has both the vision of the ideal and the sensitivity to detect when this is not yet realized and what still needs to be done. It is a hard taskmaster, stern and unrelenting. It admires perfection above all things and, like the Driver, its closest ally among subpersonalities, is the internalized voice of all the taskmasters you have had in the past. Your Inner Judge is constantly measuring whatever you do against a whole list of criteria inherited from the past – and awarding marks out of ten.

If you are fortunate enough to have a sensible Critic your work will always be of reasonable standard. Its ability to make you feel bad about yourself when you step out of line will ensure that you behave in a civilized way, both avoiding excess and treating other people in the way you yourself would like to be treated. You will probably be cultured, and something of a connoisseur of fine things. In your work it provides you with the distancing necessary for objective and dispassionate self-appraisal, the dissatisfaction with your performance that takes you 'back to the drawing-board' time and time again, or makes you practise until it tells you that at last you have got it right. It is a sensible Inner Critic, as well of course as talent (which the Critic will refine), that makes the difference between the gifted amateur and the true professional.

'Critic' energy is needed for

- professional criticism
- judging
- prosecuting and defending
- examining
- debating
- correcting
- analysing
- comparing
- research
- detection
- quality control
- fault-finding

THE SADISTIC INNER CRITIC

Model

- Judge Jeffries (the 'Hanging Judge')

This negative Inner Critic is more intent on finding fault than detecting faults – and more concerned with judging them rather than putting them right. People with strongly developed negative Critics will never have a high opinion of themselves, for their self-esteem will have been eroded long ago under the succession of put-downs dealt out by this subpersonality. It is always comparing you with other people. They are always 'more' than you: more intelligent, attractive, successful, confident, loving, lovable, et cetera, et cetera, et cetera.

What makes the negative Critic so lethal to our peace of mind is that it is the sharpest and most perceptive of them all. Too often what it picks on within us really is something we need to work on. But it does not tell us that. Rather it condemns us out of hand for not measuring up NOW to its ideals of how we should be. It can be relentless and uncaring in its total disregard for whether we are strong enough to take what is has to tell us or not. If it is particularly reckless and is not balanced by redeeming subpersonalities like Playful Child or Parent it could actually persuade the Ego to pass the death sentence on itself and commit suicide. It is more often content merely to cause depression, lack of confidence, and despair.

It is the most cunning of all our subpersonalities, and creeps up on us, sometimes in disguise. One of its favourite disguises is that of self-improvement. What this really means for the Critic is that we must not rest until we have achieved Superman or Superwoman status together with Cosmic Consciousness. We may spend much time, money and effort trying to compensate for the feelings of inferiority that nag us day in, day out, for this subpersonality is like a bulldog, never letting up since it has got its teeth into us. We will work on ourselves with the same relentlessness: body-building, dieting, cosmetic surgery, therapy groups, meditation for hours on end . . . But even when we have the bulging pectorals and biceps, the streamlined bust or cute little nose, and can assert ourselves or play the enlightenment game with the best of them, still, the Critic whispers inside us, 'You still aren't ENOUGH. You should be more loving, involved, unselfish, committed etc., etc.' The favourite word of the Critic is 'should'; its favourite pastime is comparing: 'Look at X (and Y and Z'). So you bend over backwards trying to imitate Bob Geldof or Mother Teresa to all and sundry until either you give up in exhaustion or some other subpersonality decides that enough is enough — and your Inner Critic triumphantly unmasks you as being phoney all along.

There is no way you can win with the negative Critic for it is much cleverer than you. All you can do is try to be aware of when it is getting at you and the disguises it comes in, some of them very noble and beautiful. Its voice, however, will give it away. For there is never any love in it, and no humour. So listen carefully next time it tells you that you are not OK as you are — and draw on your Nourishing Parent and Playful Child to tell it where to get off. Otherwise you may well find yourself torturing yourself in the name of religion or the search for enlightenment. This could include wearing a hair shirt or being subjected to self-flagellation for your sins, or retiring to an Indian ashram to meditate endlessly while you are eaten alive by mosquitoes, amoebas or red ants. Or all of them, depending on how confused your Ego has become at the hands of your Inner Critic. For, ultimately, if this perfectionist subpersonality is allowed to pull your strings, it could drive you perfectly mad.

THE DANCE OF THE SELVES
Bonding and polarizing

It should be apparent by now that there is more to each of us than meets the 'I'. As we become more aware of our selves, we uncover different layers of them. Subpersonalities, like the cells of our bodies, become more and more differentiated and more and more specialized as we grow. We have seen how the different aspects of the Child give rise in turn to more sophisticated subpersonalities which either develop to protect its vulnerability, or to express in more specific forms its capacity for feeling, playing or seeing the romantic and magical sides of the world. As we grow older, these subpersonalities proliferate until we are verily, each of us, a crowd. Which habits, quirks, eccentricities we have depend on who is in that crowd. There may be the one that only likes his eggs underdone or sunny side up, one that is absent-minded or always mislays her spectacles, one that is terribly house-proud and can't stand untidiness in any shape or form. Or there may by a subpersonality that expects everyone else to watch the television programme it wants to see (and sulks if they won't let it), or likes to leave socks or undies on the floor in the bathroom, or always picks its nose when perplexed. We take our 'crowd' with us everywhere we go (for they are who we are), including into our relationships. If any of these subpersonalities are not appreciated by any subpersonality in a partner, we may have a domestic squabble on our hands. Depending on the strength of the aversion, it could even be grounds for divorce due to 'mutual incompatibility'.

Relationships become much more intelligible when we see them as energy transactions, in terms of the attraction or repulsion, the expectations and the needs of different subpersonalities in each of the parties involved in the relationship. Why, for example, are you in love with or married to this particular person? Or, perhaps, falling out of love, separated or divorced — perhaps on the grounds of 'irreconcilable differences'? Here are a few examples of the dance of the selves, how subpersonalities bond with each other (producing attraction or harmonious relating) or polarize against each other (producing conflict).

GOOD FATHER–OBEDIENT DAUGHTER

Jane is an example of a person whose Vulnerable Child chose her husband for her. Her father had died when she was very young and she barely remembered him. Her mother had never really recovered from the shock of her husband's sudden death in an industrial accident and became something of a hypochondriac. Often, on coming home from school, Jane would find the doctor there, and her mother in bed with one of her 'turns', sometimes so apparently serious as to necessitate her removal to hospital for observation. On these occasions Jane's older sister would look after the house and prepare the meals for the two of them. But the sister had been called on to do this too many times, had to take time off from her job too often to look after her younger sister, and resented it. She felt her mother should 'pull herself together' and would tell her this when, as usual, she came home again, having been discharged from hospital after a few days. For Jane, this meant that she always had the uncomfortable feeling that she was a burden to her mother and her sister. Like Sam's, her Child shrank from adding to their burden by asking for anything for itself, and developed a strong Pleaser to try to lighten their burden so that she should not feel so guilty. Jane's Vulnerable Child had never had the experience of really feeling held.

She had virtually given up on men, who always seemed to be only out for sex — which was not really what she needed for her Child. On the occasions when she had given in to their insistence she had been disappointed, for it had seemed empty and meaningless, and she had been left feeling lonelier than before . . . She was only dimly aware that her real needs were for warmth and holding, and that it was difficult to get these without having to trade sex for them. All she was in touch with was that somehow it 'didn't feel right'. Until she met Malcolm.

He was older than her usual boyfriends, more mature, very 'together' and used to taking charge, for he had built up a successful carpet-cleaning business from nothing and was in charge of a team of employees. He was everything her Little Girl had longed for from a father: a man she could look up to, feel safe with, warm and loving, above all, holding . . .

Jane was clear that this time she wanted more than a short affair, and put the Pleaser to work to convince Malcolm that she would have a lot to offer as a wife. She put energy into looking good, being a good listener, suggesting she cook for him at his place as a change from being taken out to dinner, flattering and charming him in subtle ways . . . Now that he had established his business he was ready to settle down, even though a part of him was used to being free and doing what he liked, when he liked. But Jane was pretty, charming and they got on well and had good times together. The Good Father in him became progressively bonded (or 'hooked' by) the waif-like quality of Jane's Vulnerable Child (because it made him feel strong, protective, manly) and by her Obedient Daughter (that satisfied his need to be in control). So his Good Father subpersonality was the one that was primarily responsible for making him propose.

At first things went well. Jane's Child was at last experiencing what it was like to be held in the arms of a man she could trust to be there for her, and felt safe within the boundaries of permanence that marriage seemed to promise. She began to play out her own version of Obedient Daughter to meet the expectations she sensed from Malcolm.

But, little by little, Jane began to be aware of her husband's growing irritation with her. He had begun to experience her as very demanding, not of things, but of his energy. She was always there, needing attention: when he came home from work, when he was trying to read the newspaper, to take a nap or just to relax and be with himself. Drained at work, he began to feel more drained at home, and to resent his wife for not respecting his space, allowing him time for himself.

But space between herself and this father figure was something that Jane's Vulnerable Child could not tolerate, for she had been too long separated from her real Daddy and was hungry for contact. The more she sensed Malcolm withdrawing, the more anxious she became — and the more she pursued him with cups of tea, with inquiries about nothing of importance, with unwelcome fondling. He did not sense the desperation behind her caresses, only their intrusiveness. The part of him that needed to be free and had viewed his marriage with misgiving started to be activated again. He started going for drinks after work with his employees, coming home late for dinner.

As Jane's Vulnerable Child became more and more threatened by what it interpreted as her husband's desertion, it started to rely less on the Pleaser and more on her Protector-Controller to keep her man at home. She stopped placating and started demanding instead. Her laying down the law, telling Malcolm how she expected him to behave, constantly nagging him, made her in his eyes become the Bad Mother and activated his Rebellious Son. As they became more and more polarized into these roles their life together became a locking of horns of two subpersonalities, for this is what polarization is. It is also the source of quarrels, manipulations and taking revenge, as each subpersonality figures out its next move in the struggle to be allowed to be itself. The next move for Malcolm's Rebellious Son subpersonality (teaming up with his Free Spirit?) was to make him succumb to the seduction of one of the girls at work who had been after him for some time. He started to come home later and later, smelling not only of alcohol but also of perfume. The counter-move of Jane's Protector-Controller was to make her move out, which served the double purpose of removing her Child from exposure to more traumas and manipulating her husband into feeling guilty.

At the moment she has 'gone home to mother' (her sister also has married), and Malcolm is still 'carrying on' with his affair, though, predictably, this is fizzling out. It had been fuelled largely by a subpersonality that was no longer being provoked. Jane and Malcolm have agreed on the telephone to stay away from each other for a while until 'we are sure of how we feel'. What they are in fact saying is that this particular dance of subpersonalities is over for the time being, or at least that they are 'sitting this one out' until they feel like dancing together again. Which particular dance they will perform next depends on whether new subpersonalities are coming to the fore and wanting to take over. Otherwise it will be a repeat performance when they get back together again and nothing will have changed. Jane's 'Victim' subpersonality is making a strong bid and, providing it can re-activate Malcolm's 'Good Father' again, stands a good chance of keeping him where she wants him, this time through guilt. But it depends on how ruthless his 'Free Spirit' is, whether it will be tough enough to insist on a clean break. If it does, Jane's Vulnerable Child may give up totally on finding somebody she can depend on to hold her and get more firmly entrenched behind her Victim (a subpersonality we shall be meeting in the next chapter). As Jane gets older, this Victim may differentiate into other subpersonalities, for example Man-hater, or Old Maid (the bitter variety). Or even Hypochondriac, just like Mother.

The primal bonding pattern is between a child and its mother. It is our first experience of love, of nourishment, of support (and deprivation) and will profoundly affect the ways in which we perceive the world and ourselves in later life as adults. For the infant, its mother *is* its world, and out of its experience of Good Mother (giving) and Bad Mother (witholding) come the first shocks to its omnipotence and the seeds of later vulnerabilities, needs and expectations in intimate relationships. As a young child one learns how to manipulate as well as how to please in order to make up for one's lack of stature in the family. Depending on whether one is an only child or has siblings, one either assumes one will always be the centre of attention, that one has to compete for it, or resign oneself to lack of it, in a large family for example. The special ways in which the Child succeeds in getting what it wants to harden into habits, automatic ways of relating that as adults we fall back on what Erikson called configurationally similar circumstances — situations that *feel* the same as when we were children.

CONTROLLING PARENT– REBELLIOUS SON/DAUGHTER

Adolescence adds further layers of subpersonalities arising out of the adolescent's needs for separating from close parental control, assertion of individuality and finding peer groups. The more vulnerable the Inner Child, the harder it is to separate from the parents, to leave the nest and create a home of one's own, especially if the parent(s) are over-protective or themselves too vulnerable to tolerate what they feel is abandonment by their offspring. If, however, the protecting-controlling aspects of the parents have made the Child feel sufficiently safe and allow it to leave home without sacrificing their love and support, the transition from Dependent Child to Independent Adult is likely to be smooth.

The Rebellious Son and Rebellious Daughter subpersonalities one so often sees in teenagers may be the only energies they can summon up to counteract guilt-slinging or rigid boundary-setting of parents reluctant to relinquish their power (often from a lack of trust that their offspring's Protector-Controllers are sufficiently developed to allow them to venture forth yet from the nest). As is the case with all subpersonalities, these Rebels can go 'over the top' and enjoy the 'high' of rebellion for its own sake.

This type of polarization is often fought out in the classroom. Built into the job of being a schoolteacher is having to cope with the hostility of some children for whom rebellion has become, if not a way of life, at least their only way of relating to anybody who appears in the slightest way to be a parental figure. If the teacher's Protector-Controller then becomes threatened and activated by what it perceives as Rebellious Sons and Daughters in the class, polarization happens. And, as always with polarization, the opposing energies become entrenched in their positions, assailing each other with the weapons at their disposal. In the blackboard jungle, such negative polarization between Controlling Parent and Rebellious Child can lead children to actually assault staff (or vandalize their cars or school property). This has caused some disarray in the opposing camp. The Collective Protector-Controller whose voice is heard in the teachers' union is obviously both concerned about its inability to protect its members and confused as to the boundaries it has the right to insist upon for adequately controlling the Rebellious Children whom they must try to teach.

Such polarization of the energy of Rebellious Sons and Daughters against what they see as images of the over-Controlling Parent contributes to creating jungles, not only of our schools, but of our inner cities as well. Rebellious Children will tend to see the law as the instrument of repression rather than something which is there for their own protection. Flouting it may well be a necessary requirement for feeling part of a peer group, and like the justice of the law, such flouting must not only be done, but must be seen to be done. And one has only to notice (how could one not?) omnipresent graffiti and vandalized telephone booths to note that it is indeed done with a vengeance. And not only to property whose defence the law avows to uphold, but to anything or anyone that carries the hated parental energy. This could be any aspect of the Establishment, its traditions, its mores, its Church, its Government. For the Rebellious Son/Daughter energy has fired more reformers, heretics and revolutionaries throughout history than any other subpersonality, and has often been the harbinger of change in society. This dynamic is often reflected in the language of both contemporaries who lived through these changes and later historians who chronicled them: Luther versus 'Mother Church', Mrs Pankhurst versus Winston Churchill and the 'paternalistic' Government of which he was an influential member . . . The shattering results of such polarization included not only the Reformation in the sixteenth century, but also broken shop windows at Harrods, targets for irate Suffragettes who vented their frustration so regularly that the windows had to be boarded up.

The perpetration of violence by the young on the old may be only partly explained by the vulnerability of the old people which makes pensioners too often the targets of cowardly housebreakers and muggers. The sheer viciousness of some of these attacks would suggest that the unfortunate victims are the targets for an energy that has turned demonic in its blind rage and callous contempt for anyone and anything old. But then, if you see life as a jungle and there is a predator inside your head, the old and frail of any species will be the easiest prey.

That Rebellious Son and Rebellious Daughter are subpersonalities is obvious from the fact that they make way, when the occasion demands, for other subpersonalities. The mugger does not mug his own parents, is probably a good friend to one or more of his peers, capable of showing tenderness to his girlfriend or wife. He cares as well as scares, unless he is totally schizoid or psychopathic. The female of this species of rebellious subpersonality turned anti-social, who might be expressing herself as a drug-abuser, pusher, or runner or a prostitute may well also be a loving mother to her child. And, as we shall see, transformation of a subpersonality can happen, as in the case of the Prodigal Son, an early example of a Rebel redeemed. Sometimes the lines between rebellion and obedience become blurred: atrocities are being carried out today by terrorists who would consider themselves acting in the interests of or avenging their Motherland or Fatherland, or loyally serving a leader seen as the Good Father.

It is not only the biological changes that take place during adolescence that make this such a turbulent time. This is one of the transition periods in our lives when who we are and will become is being painfully hammered out on the anvil of instinctual drives and parental and societal pressures. What are being forged are some of the subpersonalities that will help us cope with the challenges with which this period of our lives faces us. We are expected to find our level socially, professionally and sexually — which most often, if one follows the path of Obedient Son and Daughter rather than that of their Rebellious siblings, means 'fitting in'.

MACHO MAN v LIBERATED WOMAN

As Wilhelm Reich believed, some of our heaviest conditioning is to do with our gender and sexuality. As a result, we identify with the subpersonalities that express these and tend to feel threatened very easily if either our gender or our sexuality is invalidated in any way. These subpersonalities can therefore influence bonding in very specific ways — and cause explosive polarization in order to protect a threatened sense of identity.

In some countries men are heavily conditioned to develop a dominant male subpersonality, which, for want of a better word, we will refer to as 'macho'. One thinks particularly of South America and the Arab world, but it is also common in men brought up in countries whose early settlers needed the toughness, aggressiveness and endurance of this energy to survive at all, such as Australia and South Africa. The 'macho' energy is well suited to pioneering, building homes, to defending territory and protecting women and children. One would not therefore be surprised to find this subpersonality with its rough language and camaraderie in places where predominantly male occupations are being carried out: at building sites, in the armed forces and police (to judge at least from the recurring stereotypes of macho detectives in television series). We are talking here about attitudes, not about class. Machos are to be found in all walks of life, including boardrooms, universities – even, apparently, the Church. What they have in common is a deep suspicion, if not fear, of women, from which stems a determination to keep them in their place – usually the kitchen or bed, but definitely somewhere at home, preferably rearing children. How the energy is channelled determines whether or not subpersonalities appear as positive or negative. And one of the ways this energy can be channelled negatively is when it rides rough-shod over the other, non-macho subpersonalities, whether one's own or other people's.

In those countries where women have succeeded in challenging the male's exclusive right to dominance, whether within marriage or the professions, the Macho's confused inflexibility is forcing the male Ego to rethink its relationship with the subpersonality which for centuries regarded women as yet another territory to be dominated. Once conquered, she became thereafter his possession to be ruled as he wished. In the Middle Ages the cult of the Virgin Mary combined with the new ideal of 'courtly love' of the Troubadours to soften their *machismo*, at least in Europe. Yet the only subpersonalities a woman could express with the approval of her man was that of Mother or Wife, with the added energy of the Virgin that kept her impenetrable by other men and therefore very patently still her husband's possession. This, remember, was the age of the chastity belt, and a most fitting symbol it was of the bonding between medieval Macho and his Virginal Wife-Mother.

That centuries past witnessed much witch-burning is more evidence of this fear of the power of women. Like any other unacknowledged energy, it was driven underground. No doubt some of the women who were burnt dabbled in sorcery and love potions, the only way they could gain access to any sense of their own power. The fact that their executions were cheered by other women as well as men is understandable: not only were they not in touch with their own female power but feared the reprisals that any expression of it would bring. The only concession of Macho to the power of woman was and is under her aspect as the Mother. Her role in the home was unchallenged, though it might on occasion be ignored or forgotten under the influence of drink, for one of the attributes of the Macho subpersonality is that it likes (or has to pretend to like) to get drunk. (Test your Macho rating: how many pints can you knock down before you fall down?)

One of the main themes of this century has been the progressive emancipation of more and more of women's subpersonalities. University education allowed the Intellectual Woman to come into her own and train for professions other than the motherly ones like nursing or nannying. The suffragettes freed the energies of the Political Woman in spite of male opposition. However, before they were considered sensible enough to qualify for the vote they had to prove that they could 'do a man's job' during the Great War. (Presumably, the all-male Houses of Parliament considered that if you could make a bomb, even though you were a woman, you must be OK). In a few countries the Stateswoman has been allowed to appear again after a long eclipse, to take up from where the great Queens and Empresses of the past left off.

But until recently the Sexual Woman has been a source of confusion to both men and women, fraught with double standards and therefore double messages. This subpersonality has too often been publicly abhorred by men as the Whore (but privately enjoyed by many). However, in the Ancient World, she took her place amid the other Goddesses. The energy carried by Aphrodite and Venus, except by poets, has never been honoured in the Christian World in the same way as the energies carried by woman's Mother and the Virgin aspects (the latter energy being carried most obviously by the Nun, respectfully addressed as 'Sister', taking her vow of chastity together with that of obedience to her 'Mother' Superior). For women who have been educated in a convent school particularly, there may be little or no guidance — and certainly no suitable model — for her Aphrodite subpersonality to follow.

That Aphrodite is more liberated and integrated in our time than ever before is probably due to more effective methods of birth control rather than to a growth of respect for this Goddess subpersonality on the part of the Macho subpersonality in men. Indeed, they are often threatened by this Goddess when she awakes to her power — and take to their heels. And their Protector-Controller is not merely being paranoid if they do. For, as Congreve made Zara observe in *The Way of The World*:

> Heaven has no rage like love to hatred turned,
> Nor Hell a fury like a woman scorned.

But then, this could be said, not only of Aphrodite, but of any subpersonality that is not honoured. Man's Liberation, like Woman's Liberation (and indeed of any other form of liberation), lies in the direction of freeing the energy locked away in subpersonalities that, because of social conditioning, are being suppressed or disowned. This means that personal growth for women will tend more to involve discovering, acknowledging and integrating their Power subpersonalities, and for men, having the courage and the honesty to admit to and allow expression of their more vulnerable sides, their Child energies. The resistance to this is the resistance to what one has been conditioned to label as 'masculinity' or 'femininity', rather than to the energies, potentially available to us all, man or woman.

The Macho mentality, aided by popular fiction and much of what came out of Hollywood, imposed its own stereotyped bonding pattern as the norm, thereby straitjacketing *everybody*, including heterosexual men. The sign of the times however is that Macho Man is now having to make room for other male subpersonalities to develop instead of being crowded out or disowned. James Bond has become more like a real man and less like a Real Man. He is now shown capable of finer feelings than those only appropriate to Super Stud — Licensed to Kill. That the new James Bonding pattern is monogamous rather than promiscuous might well be in deference to post-AIDS box-office requirements, but in another sense it is still a sign of the times. Men are themselves being liberated from the compulsive Casanova subpersonality and allowing their softer and more caring sides to be seen without feeling unmanned. We may even look forward to 007 actually being seen washing dishes, baby-sitting, changing nappies in between assignments. After all, this is what many men have to do these days when the wife is also a breadwinner (and, in an age of unemployment, sometimes *the* breadwinner) in the family.

GOOD MOTHER–OBEDIENT SON

Not all men, however, have a strongly developed Macho subpersonality. In some relationships the woman is definitely the dominant partner. Whether or not these types of relationships are happy ones depends very much, as usual, on whether their respective subpersonalities bond or polarize. If the male has a strong Dominant Male subpersonality their life together is likely to be about who is to be Top Dog (or Top Bitch — and bitching there will certainly be plenty of). If she wins and he gives up for good we are then in the Henpeck Bonding so popular with cartoonists. If his Dominant Male has merely been driven underground, it will seethe there with the resentment one so often hears behind the muttered 'Yes, Dear', 'No, Dear'. Hopefully, this subpersonality will not sour into the Demonic as in so many cases of wife-murder and lead him to quietly poison her, Crippen style, or attack her in a frenzy.

However, in many cases, these relationships in which

the female is the dominant partner do seem to work. Indeed, the partners often bond to mutual satisfaction, even when the female plays Bad Mother (as in sado-masochistic relationships) provided the male has a subpersonality which enjoys the passive role, even though he complains about it (which could be part of the enjoyment).

The Good Mother–Obedient Son type of relationship, however, even in an age where women are able to allow their power sides to show, is probably rarer than the pairing of Good Father–Obedient Daughter, as, for example, in the case of Jane and Malcolm. It will tend to evolve whenever the female is manifestly stronger or less vulnerable than her partner, for example if he is an invalid or handicapped, or much younger. This bonding sometimes happens between nurses and their patients who get emotionally involved while the man is in hospital and later marry. It is interesting to surmise why the opposite coupling — of male doctor and female patient — should not only be seen by, for example, the Press as unromantic but is unfailingly pilloried as unprofessional and exploitative. This would suggest that, because doctors carry the aura of Good Father, this type of bonding offends because it feels like an infringement of the incest taboo, irrespective of who actually seduced whom.

The above are only a few of the possible bonding patterns. Under the generic umbrellas of Parent-Child and Male-Female there are many more different types of bonding possible according to the differing subpersonalities of the partners in the relationship. The way lovers refer to or address each other is often an indication of the way in which they have bonded together. This can range from the affectionate 'Mother' and 'Dad' used by the elderly couple to the impersonal third party 'Mr' and 'Mrs'. What they call each other when they are quarrelling is also a clear indication of how they polarize. Harmony and bliss between partners depends ultimately on how many of their respective subpersonalities mesh with each other — or cannot tolerate each other's existence. The greater the aversion, the clearer the polarization into warring camps.

And then it becomes a case, not of 'May the best win', but 'May the more strident, powerful, or manipulative subpersonality win'.

TYPE CASTING
Psychological types

The Child, Parent, Pleaser, Driver and Critic are subpersonalities which everybody has, for the Child we were born with and the others, as we have seen, developed in the process of our upbringing and in the interests of helping us survive (and, perhaps, survive our upbringing). The particular way in which these energies manifest in us depends on such variables as our inherited tendencies and our conditioning. By 'conditioning' I mean the expectations we experienced as coming from our environment and what was considered acceptable or not from significant Others. These expectations were reinforced by approval or disapproval, reward or punishment, being shown love or having it withdrawn. Our heredity will probably have decided into which of Jung's categories of psychological types we come, whether extroverted or introverted, more inclined to experience primarily through the functions of thought, feeling, sensation or intuition.

One of these will be your 'superior' function and will be like a 'fat' (well-developed) subpersonality that you use a lot in relating to the world and tend to be identified with. The other three functions will be relatively undeveloped in you unless you work to develop them, and so Jung called them 'inferior' functions. Not that they themselves are really inferior, but you don't value them as highly as you do your own superior function, and the particular ways of perceiving reality that the others represent do not come naturally to you. Opposite types are: thinking versus feeling and sensing versus intuitive.

It might not be an overstatement to suggest that the Child is parent to *all* the subpersonalities that develop in us as a result of heredity and conditioning (including the Parent), in that it is the only one that is there from the very beginning. Milton expressed this in *Paradise Regained*:

> The childhood shows the man,
> As morning shows the day.

Or, as Wordsworth put it a century and a half later in *My Heart Leaps Up*:

> The Child is father of the Man.

Since it is the subpersonality closest to our essence, one would expect to find the Child connected in some way with the four 'essential' psychological functions. The Child may not be obvious in the emotional coolness of the intellectual, but this is misleading, for not only is rationalization often a defence against experiencing feelings or vulnerability, but the true intellectual likes to 'play' with ideas and enjoys the cut and thrust of sharp debate. The archetypal 'feeler' among all subpersonalities is the Vulnerable Child, and some of the subpersonalities described below as expressions of the sensing and intuitive functions are also aspects of the Playful Child and the Magical Child respectively.

Depending on which 'type' you are, you may have one of the following subpersonalities so fully developed that you identify with it and take it for granted, or undeveloped because it is an energy carried by your opposite, 'inferior' function. Remember that the opposite energy is always there in you, perhaps only as your potential, a seed or an embryo. Here are a few.

THE INTELLECTUAL (INTROVERTED THINKING TYPE)

Models:

- academics
- the 'swot'
- a computer

Things Intellectual subpersonalities are good at

- swotting
- lecturing
- philosophy
- arguing
- debating
- prosecuting or defending in court
- report-writing
- classifying
- programming
- computing
- crosswords

The Intellectual subpersonality does not feel comfortable unless it understands the whys and wherefores of things. It relies heavily on logic and memory, on classifying and compartmentalizing to feel it 'has a good grasp' of a subject, has 'got on top of it' and is 'breaking its back'. These turns of speech highlight the aggressive, penetrating quality of logic and intellect, the *male* energy carried by this subpersonality, whether it appears in a man or a woman. It often succeeds in getting us to the heart of the matter, but since it lacks the sensitivity of more heart-centred energies, it often does this without perhaps even being aware of the pain its surgical precision might be occasioning in others. It is more tuned into its own ideas than to other people's feelings — or other subpersonalities. It is strong on words but thin on feeling (its opposite psychological type) and intuition. Unless there are other energies around to soften it, this subpersonality can make for hard, unfeeling men and unfeminine, 'bluestocking' women. Yet it undoubtedly makes for success in our culture, which sets such a high premium on it that its educational system is almost exclusively geared to fostering it. This is also why there are more obvious examples of this type of psychological function around than of the others. Since the Intellectual lacks a developed feeling function, this type when at home tends to be a

RATIONAL PARENT

Models:

- Head-master/headmistress
- The 'benevolent despots' in eighteenth century Europe.

Things Rational Parents say

- 'Why on earth should you feel like that?'
- 'Now what seems to be the problem here?'
- 'I believe that children should be brought up to be . . . '
- 'Don't be such a crybaby'
- 'Now pull yourself together'.

The Rational Parent has, in common with the Intellectual, an almost exclusive reliance on reason to illuminate the way out of any uncomfortable situation – which usually means an emotional outburst of some sort – rather in the same way as he would make for the subway Exit sign to escape from the rush-hour free-for-all. I say 'he', for Rational Parent is most usually a father trying to be Good Father, or a boss trying to be Reasonable Boss. When you are under pressure in any way from your family (or your employees/secretary/board/shareholders) he will be the subpersonality who helps you try to bring the dissidents 'to see reason', 'to be reasonable'.

The Rational Parent is dependable, civilized, fair and well-meaning and usually makes a popular boss. If you are a father the same applies. But this subpersonality may well at times provoke rebellion in your children, for they may often not feel that their feelings are really seen and acknowledged by you. This cool, detached Parent subpersonality tends to be strong in men who have been taught to deny their own Vulnerable Child in the best 'Boys don't cry' tradition, to disown their softer feelings as 'sissy'. Inevitably (we shall be seeing why later), he will tend to be ill at ease with displays of distress (especially from his sons) and baffled by rebellion if the cause is not immediately obvious. And even more baffled when his attempts to find the reason seem to provoke even more distress or rebellion. He will be unaware that it is precisely this detachment that is fuelling both.

Child: Can I stay home from school today?
Rational Parent: No, of course not. Why?
Child: I don't feel so good.
Rational Parent: You said that yesterday.
Child: I felt bad yesterday too.
Rational Parent: Of course you didn't. It was because you didn't want to go to school. It's called 'malingering'.
Child: But . . .
Rational Parent: And if you do that when you grow up you'll lose your job!
Child: But I have a pain in my tummy.
Rational Parent: No you don't. You only think you do.
Child: (wincing and holding belly) But I do!
Rational Parent: Daddy doesn't want to go to work today either but *he* has to. Don't you want to grow up to be a responsible citizen like your Daddy? Somebody other people can rely on . . .

(Child at this point collapses, screaming, to the floor. Alarmed, Rational Parent summons the family doctor who diagnoses acute appendicitis. Child is now in hospital recovering from emergency operation. Rational Parent stays home from work, recovering from shock.)

THE IMPERSONAL (EXTROVERTED THINKING TYPE)

Outer model of the Impersonal

- a vending machine

When you are on the receiving end of somebody else's Impersonal subpersonality you will feel it straight away. You will be treated in a cool, detached manner and tend to experience the other person as aloof and somewhat remote. You sense that they are feeding you with only as much attention or energy as is necessary to keep you engaged in polite conversation or to complete the transaction in progress between you. Depending on which of your own subpersonalities is activated by finding yourself confronted by the Impersonal in another person, you may consider them professional, dignified, cold, or 'snooty', And, if one of your emotional, volatile or needy subpersonalities is upfront, infuriating (for you may feel as if you are up against a brick wall), or unnerving (for they make you feel gauche and awkward).

The Impersonal is very much in evidence on formal occasions, and the more formal the occasion ('State anything': opening of Parliament, banquets, visits) the more *de rigueur* the Impersonal energy. Developing this subpersonality is part of the training of many in the public eye, for they could not do the job they do without it. As its name suggests, the Impersonal is for many their *persona*, the professional mask which serves to conceal their personality. Revealing their true personality would be a distraction for everybody (including themselves) from the performance or service in which they are engaged. The Impersonal often has a survival function in that it is economical of energy, and thus saves the Ego from getting drained by putting more into the job than is strictly necessary to do it well. Its detachment is also useful if the job we have to do is particularly unpleasant, potentially hazardous or emotionally arduous. It is the one that most helps us remain helpful and polite when dealing with the public (even though we may be exhausted, or be up against difficult customers) and to 'keep our heads' in emergencies.

People who need the Impersonal subpersonality to do their job

- Royalty
- Heads of State
- judges
- chairmen of meetings
- armed forces
- police
- barristers
- doctors
- surgeons
- nurses
- ambulance men
- rescue workers
- bomb disposal experts
- firemen
- secretaries
- receptionists
- fashion models
- television newsreaders
- airline staff
- shop assistants
- toastmasters
- waiters
- civil servants
- bus conductors

THE ROMANTIC (EXTROVERTED FEELING TYPE)

Models for the energy carried by this subpersonality:

- King Arthur, Galahad, Lancelot and Co.
- the medieval troubadours
- Don Quixote
- The Three Musketeers
- Franz Liszt
- Karen Blixen
- Barbara Cartland

The Romantic is at exactly the opposite pole to the Impersonal. For this subpersonality, the worst thing one could say about anyone was that they 'had no feeling', or about a performance, that it was 'cold, had no heart in it'. For the Romantic, being able to feel, and free to express those feelings is what life (and art) is all about. It was no coincidence that the Romantic and Liberal movements were contemporary in nineteenth century Europe or that they nourished and supported each other, for each sought freedom from the restraints of the past in its own way. If this subpersonality is strong in you it will put you on the side of freedom in any shape or form. You will be impatient with the restraints that the Protector-Controller energy urges or tries to impose from within or without. The more repressive this energy is experienced to be, the more extreme the polarization of the Romantic against it. This interplay is the stuff of which the great epics and romantic novels are made, and we shall look at a few of these later on.

The Romantic sees life as a *roman*, a *romanzo*, a story or novel with himself or herself as the main character, and, preferably, with a happy or tragic ending. The Romantic often imagines the past life in which he or she was somebody famous, such as Cleopatra or Genghis Khan, or somebody special — a vestal virgin or a high priest (but never a mere slave, untouchable, or the one with the job of cleaning out the cesspits). The Romantic hankers after faraway places like Bali or Kathmandu: the farther away from the here and now, the better. The Romantic is the subpersonality of the stuff dreams are made on, and is very much an aspect of the Magical Child energy. Ideals, idealization and ideal ways of behaving figure largely in the world picture of this subpersonality, which tends to complain that things are not as they *should* be when disillusioned and forced to face things (and people) as they *are*. Blanche in *A Streetcar Named Desire* was an example of a Romantic having a hard time trying to reconcile the two.

The Romantic is above all fascinated by the idea of love in any shape or form: courtly love, eternal love, predestined love, unrequited love, star-cross'd love — to name but a few variations on what non-Romantics would call the 'boy meets girl' theme. Predictably, Romantics never 'have sex' — they 'make love' instead, preferably after having overcome all odds. They enjoy secrets, intrigue, unconventionality, eloping and, if the last is not possible, worshipping from afar.

This subpersonality will make you

- write or read poetry
- read romances and historical novels
- enjoy candlelit dinners
- spend a lot of time arranging flowers just right
- idealize (and personalize) nature in all its forms
- an individualist to the point of eccentricity
- an outlandish dresser
- enjoy being somewhat outrageous.

Music is usually very important to the Romantic, who can really get lost in it and often learns to play an instrument in adolescence, a time when this subpersonality usually develops (if it is to develop at all).

Favourite music of teenage Romantics

- Romantic piano concertos (especially Grieg's and the Rachmaninov No. 2)
- Beethoven (played really loud à la *Clockwork Orange*)
- anything by Chopin or Tchaikovsky
- Sibelius and Mahler (for the more sophisticated adolescent Romantic, like Adrian Mole).

The Romantic's enjoyment of classical music is often enhanced by associating fantasies or 'programmes' with the piece being listened to, usually pastoral, idyllic, epic or tragic, and they appreciate the composers' help in supplying inspiring names, such as 'Eroica', 'Revolutionary', 'Unfinished' or 'Romeo and Juliet' and '1812'. In the absence of any such assistance, however, they can always fall back on their own imagination and be the conductor of the orchestra, the concert pianist, or both. (Either that or they hate classical music and only ever listen to pop, in which case they will fantasize that they are pop stars).

Some of the favourite films of grown-up Romantics

- Camille
- Gone With The Wind
- Camelot
- My Fair Lady
- The Sound of Music
- Dr Zhivago

They may see these films over and over again and brush away a tear at the end – each time.

VICTIM (INTROVERTED FEELING TYPE)

Model for the Victim energy

- Donald Duck
- Moaning Minnie
- The Old Woman Who Lived In A Shoe
- Jonah

Our Victim (and we all have, or potentially have this subpersonality) is pulling our strings whenever we blame someone else rather than sharing our feelings with them, or complain about a situation without trying to do anything about it. In fact, the Victim never allows us to *do* anything, for the last thing it wants is for us to realize our power to change things for the better, or to realize that it is our own responsibility to do so. If our Ego allows the Victim to manipulate it in this way, we will in turn try to manipulate others into feeling guilty or taking responsibility for us.

This subpersonality sees itself rather in the position of the Vulnerable Child unable to protect itself. Therefore, when it becomes a Hurt Child (and Victim is always terribly easily hurt) it reacts against what it feels to have been a dereliction of duty on the part of those whose responsibility it is to look after it. So it either gets depressed (sulks) or angry with (blames) the nearest responsible person who could remotely be saddled with the role of Protecting Parent. In the absence of a suitable parent, it may have a go at Life instead, but usually does not get as much satisfaction out of this.

Like all our subpersonalities, Victim has a survival value. Some people have in fact managed to survive all their lives with the help of other people whose Good Parent, kindly but unaware, has been 'hooked' by a determined and credible victim into a more or less permanent bonding. But if other subpersonalities are beginning to grow restive with the dependent and powerless status a full-blown Victim subpersonality imposes on the Ego, they may well persuade the latter to get a few clues on cutting fatso down to size by consulting my book *Take Charge of Your Life: How Not To Be A Victim* (Thorsons, 1988).

The Victim is one of the most easily identifiable subpersonalities, for its tone of voice is quite distinctive. It can be heard clearly behind some of the expressions it commonly employs, such as:

- '*You* made me do it (feel, think, say it)'
- 'I had no choice'
- 'I can't tell you how much you have hurt me'
- 'After all I've done for you. . . '
- Why does this always have to happen to *me*?'
- 'People have no consideration these days'
- 'I was just minding my own business when. . . '
- 'Just my luck'
- 'But it fell to pieces in my hands!'
- 'Why *do* they put things there for people to trip over?'

THE FIXER (INTROVERTED SENSING TYPE)

NB: Do not confuse this subpersonality with Drug Addict.

Models

- your bank manager
- Lady Chatterley's Lover
- Mrs Beeton
- Don Juan

This is an energy you need to

- DIY
- mend a fuse
- run a household
- build practically anything
- handle your own finances
- be a stockbroker
- run a farm
- be a vet
- be a mechanic or an engineer

Intellectuals and Romantics alike are often viewed with either suspicion or contempt by this subpersonality which considers them as 'airy-fairy', 'in their heads' or seeing life through rose-coloured spectacles. It values above all 'realism', 'common sense', and 'being practical'. In its negative aspect it can be cynical and manipulative in its readiness to get results by the quickest possible way. Famous examples of this psychological type were Machiavelli, the Borgias, Don Giovanni and Casanova.

This earthy energy is antagonistic to high fliers who tend to 'get above themselves', for it is rooted in the material world of things that can be seen and touched, smelled and tasted. It has little time for ideas unless it can see how they help get things done, of for feelings that only 'get in the way'. It is therefore 'good with its hands' and at rescuing damsels in distress when, for example, their car refuses to start or has broken down on the road.

Intensely pragmatic, this subpersonality believes the 'proof of the pudding is in the eating' and the criterion of a project is whether it is 'realistic' or not. This subpersonality has a homely wisdom rooted in experience that likes to express itself in proverbs, especially when it wants to bring down to earth the Romantic dreamer or idealist or deflate the pontificating Intellectual.

Things this subpersonality is fond of saying

- 'A stitch in time saves nine'
- 'A place for everything and everything in its place'
- 'None so deaf as those who won't hear'
- 'Charity begins at home'
- 'Cut your coat according to your cloth'
- 'Six of one and half a dozen of the other'
- 'Easier said than done'
- 'The early bird catches the worm'.

The Fixer tends, when homely proverbs fail, to fall back on earthier language, implying that the Intellectual's vision or the Romantic's dreams are either taurean excrement or masturbatory, or that he needs to extricate a digit. They in turn experience this down-to-earth subpersonality either as a bull in a china shop or as dull as ditchwater.

THE WARRIOR (EXTROVERTED SENSING TYPE)

Models

- Mars
- Samurai
- boxers
- army officers
- Rambo
- Bruce Lee

The most aggressively upfront of all subpersonalities, the Warrior stands for no-nonsense confrontation. When this energy starts pulling your strings the time for talking, diplomacy or politeness is past: you are spoiling for a fight.

This subpersonality is a very useful one to have in your repertoire for those times when only a show of strength will save you from being manipulated or harmed. It is the Warrior energy that *aficionados* of the martial arts tune into every time they take to the mat, or boxers when they get into the ring. It is interesting that more and more women are taking lessons in self-defence to develop this subpersonality in themselves, for it has been conventionally considered the energy appropriate only for men (with a few historical exceptions such as Boadicea). Indeed, the energy that helps to make men 'brave' or 'heroic', in a woman brands her as a 'virago', a 'hellcat' or a 'fury'. At its most creative, the Warrior enables us to stand up for ourselves and fight to defend our interests or what matters to us. Too often though it manifests as pugnaciousness (especially if the Controller has been put to sleep with alcohol) or 'fighting for the hell of it', as in tribal warfare between opposing fans (and, indeed, of members of opposing teams) at a football match. This is in fact to miss the point of much sport, which is to channel this competitive and aggressive energy in a way that *everybody* gets to enjoy (as in martial arts).

When the Warrior energy is highly esteemed in a society its men will die for honour and be easily led into war.

THE ADVENTURER (EXTROVERTED SENSING TYPE)

Models

- the Vikings
- the Conquistadores
- Scott of the Antarctic
- Thor Heyerdahl
- Sir Edmund Hillary
- Sir Francis Chichester

The adventurer is an aspect of the Playful Child energy. More than anything this subpersonality comes alive under stressful conditions which would be enough to traumatize any one of the others. It thrives on tough conditions, danger, and 'roughing it', is usually competitive and loves to break any sort of record, to be 'first' or 'fastest ever'. This subpersonality's energy is one of those that have stimulated mankind to go beyond established boundaries, to break new ground, scale new heights, explore virgin territory. It makes climbers scale mountains 'because they are there'. The more inaccessible the peak, the greater its challenge.

The Adventurer's capacity for taking risks could make for success over rivals in business, provided its tendency towards recklessness is balanced by some more intuitive energy, either in another subpersonality or within a team. But since the intuitive function is an 'inferior' one with this type, counsels of caution whether from within or without, often go unheeded, often with disastrous, even fatal results.

Not for this novelty- and excitement-seeking subpersonality your typical half-board, beach by day, disco by night package holiday. This one will take you to places out of the way and off the beaten track, enjoying meeting the natives and living the way they do. For the Adventurer, the world is one big oyster.

A similar type of energy to the Adventurer is

THE WANDERER

Models

- gypsies
- Marco Polo
- Columbus
- David Livingstone

This subpersonality is the 'gypsy in your soul'. It is characterized by a restlessness and a reluctance to stay in one place (one job, one relationship) for too long. It is usually male, and often the despair of the female, unless her own Wanderer is sufficiently well-developed to override the demands of her Child and Parent for security, a home and a family. In which case she too will don her rucksack and set off with her man (or, if they are affluent enough, jet off). Sometimes, though, this subpersonality gets its revenge for not having been given its head in adolescence and being stifled too long in a 'steady' job, by pulling strings firmly enough in middle age to cause many a 'dropout' that has startled colleagues. If the Ego identifies with this subpersonality, or its energy is not grounded by another more in touch with economic realities (for instance, the Fixer) you could end up a tramp or a bag lady. On the other hand, it might be satisfied with less than total drop out or a nomadic existence and make you feel less claustrophobic if you occasionally allow it to

- take you for long walks
- drive you off on long weekends with only a map and your toothbrush
- get you away from it all as often as you can manage it.

THE SEER (INTROVERTED INTUITIVE TYPE)

Models

- Buddha
- the Delphic Oracle
- Nostradamus
- Bhagwan Shree Rajneesh
- soothsayers
- clairvoyants
- psychotherapists
- psychic healers

This is a very useful subpersonality when well developed, for it is the part of you that knows what is really going with you and with other people. It is an inner voice, sometimes from deep in the Unconscious, one of the most aware and finely-tuned of all subpersonalities, a blending of the Child's capacity for seeing into the truth behind appearances, and the Protector's constant vigilance, its antennas probing our surroundings for hidden danger. It can, however, make us paranoid if the Vulnerable Child is too insecure, for the Protector will harness this energy for over-kill. In which case we might well become doom-prophesying Cassandras carrying placards of the 'Flee from the wrath to come' variety, or stock up our underground bunker with enough cans of food to last us until Doomsday.

It is important for those who have the Seer's gift of healing, 'second sight' or clairvoyance to have a balanced Parent (especially Nurturing Parent) subpersonality to ensure that they share their insights with people in a caring and non-manipulative way. For this subpersonality's energy has a mystique, sometimes a charisma that can lead to Ego inflation as a result of the respect, even adulation, of others in whom it is undeveloped and who therefore seek guidance or healing in some form. One can confuse the ability to 'see' with enlightenment and thus be easily led into becoming a guru or being exploited by one. Unless the knower of secrets also possesses humility and compassion, this gift can turn out to be a veritable Pandora's Box.

THE NEW AGE MAN/WOMAN (EXTROVERTED INTUITIVE TYPE)

Models

- Prince Charles
- Louise Hay
- Greenpeace
- ecologists
- organizations dedicated to preserving wildlife

Like the Seer, this is one of the most aware subpersonalities you can have. Another name for it would be the Friend of the Earth, or the Aquarian (irrespective of the birth sign of the subject). It is a subpersonality that is appearing more and more in this Age of Aquarius as concern deepens all over the planet about the damage being done to it through lack of awareness, care and caring.

This subpersonality's global awareness is linked with a compassion for all forms of life, for it sees the interdependence of these. It could lead you to want to contribute in any way you can to make this world a better place to live in: to be interested in and become informed about conservation and environmental problems such as pollution and fractures in the ozone layer; to protest against the infliction of torture, poison gas or other barbarities on fellow human beings; to support movements aimed at the preservation of endangered species (including our own).

This subpersonality tends to see everything in terms of *energy* and its changing forms, and the interconnectedness of phenomena. This model provides New Age People with a *lingua franca* with which to share with each other their particular way of working with energy and their understanding of what is happening in the world today. Some of the ways of transforming energy that they may become interested in are

- consciousness-raising techniques, for instance meditation
- 'alternative' therapies (homoeopathy, acupuncture)
- growth groups and therapies such as gestalt, transactional analysis
- relaxation techniques, for example autogenics, biofeedback.

When it is balanced, the New Age subpersonality combines the best of Magical Child and Nurturing Parent. It makes us more aware of the energy we take in and give out to others, and take responsibility for our own bodily, mental and spiritual well-being. Sometimes though, it is pressurized by the Driver and/or Critic into drastic self-improvement programmes or into trying to convert others to 'seeing the light' — and turns them off. Impatient to see its vision or project actualized, this subpersonality sometimes allies with the Driver to break through limiting ideas, red tape or established ways of proceeding. Together they will confront the less enlightened and the more conservative whom they see as obscurantists, and can be impatient with those who 'hold back'. The latter could be anyone from, for example, the more closed and resistant participants in an encounter group to the 'polluters of the environment' who deny that they are steadily poisoning the planet. Rarely is the New Age Man or Woman understood by the media. That this energy usually receives a mauling by the Press is only to be expected, for the Press represents the Sensing (preferably sensational) energy, exactly the opposite type to the Intuitive.

HIDDEN SELVES: Projected and disowned subpersonalities

Have you ever wondered why you

- ever got a crush on so-and-so
- fell in love at first sight
- feel attracted to a certain type
- can't stand other types
- continually have relationships that follow the same pattern
- feel that you are continually being misjudged
- continually seem to become the target for other people's negativity
- feel ill at ease with someone without knowing why
- attract similar sorts of experiences over and over again?

We are identified with some of our subpersonalities and think of them as 'us'. But whatever state of being we are conscious of always has its opposite in the unconscious, at least potentially, just as any light potentially can cast a shadow. Jung in fact coined the term 'shadow' for the parts of us that we are unaware of, either because they are dormant or because they have been disowned. Because we are unaware of them, our conscious Ego has no control over them. When one of these shadow energies is activated and does come to the surface it can be disturbing to our sense of 'who we are'. We might then say something like 'I don't know what came over me', or apologize because 'we weren't ourselves'. Sometimes, indeed, we may even be 'beside ourselves' or 'overcome by' something which is not usually 'in our nature'. This 'something' is a hidden subpersonality surfacing.

This may not always be unpleasant. Falling in love (and more so, infatuation) is very much about projecting onto someone of the opposite sex one's own Inner Man or Inner Woman. Psychologically, we are all both male and female, or, as Jung postulated, every male has an *anima*, every female an *animus*, a feminine and a masculine archetypal energy within them. To 'love at first sight' is to recognize (or think one does) in another person a model of ideal masculinity or femininity that one is carrying around inside oneself. This is not necessarily to do with sexuality or even with gender, but with the quality of energy. This might more usefully (because less confusing) be labelled *yang* and *yin* rather than specifically masculine or feminine. An ancient myth describes humanity as a hermaphrodite that has been cut in two and tries to become whole again by seeking out its other half.

The more rigid the cultural stereotyping of gender roles, the harder it is for cross-gender energies to find integration and expression. In our own culture, for example, we are likely to label as 'wet or unmanly' a man's expression of his Vulnerable Child or as 'bossy' or 'unfeminine' a woman's strongly developed Driver. As a result, in the process of conditioning, vulnerable and feeling subpersonalities are likely to be disowned in men and power subpersonalities in women.

Relationships are mirrors to our selves. In them we see, sometimes painfully, reflections of parts of us, of which we may hitherto have been unaware. The intimacy of close pairings tends to activate our Child energies, and make us (and our partners) feel uncomfortable with its vulnerability, neediness and fear of abandonment — and, perhaps, its omnipotent selfishness, demands and expectations. Parenting also forms a big part of relating, and throws into relief not only the Nurturing, but also the Controlling Parent who likes to lay down the law, have things done its way, and always knows the best. Much of the day-to-day interaction between lovers and spouses consists of the dance between them of their Parent and Child energies. Perhaps the best times they will have together will be when they are both Playful Children at the same time: the worst, when they are polarizing into Bad Parent/Rebellious Son or Daughter, are both Vulnerable or Omnipotent Child, or compete for the title of Most Controlling Parent. (This is known as 'quarrelling').

Loving relationships help us to grow, for we become more like that which we love. In fact, we tend to fall in love with qualities we see or sense in the other precisely because these qualities are dormant energies in ourselves that resonate with or are projected onto the partner. If we have been seeing the other person through the rose-coloured spectacles of projection we may well feel cheated when they reveal themselves in their true colours and the honeymoon is abruptly terminated. Often though, our inferior psychological function gets the chance to develop in relationships. Intellectual types learn to allow feeling and vulnerability after being repeatedly challenged by a more feeling type of partner; extroverted 'common-sensers' come to respect intuition when their partner's 'hunches' often prove right.

If, however, the opposite energy does not 'wash off', is not introjected and made one's own, once again polarization may happen. Each of the partners can become entrenched in roles, allowing the other to carry the opposite energy. Most commonly, because of conditioning, it is the man who gets stuck with the 'thinking' energy in a relationship, leaving the woman to carry his feeling function as well as her own. The more he is cut off from his own feelings, the more she is likely to feel overloaded with feeling and be impelled to act them out. Similarly, the more relentlessly down-to-earth and 'practical' one of them is, the dreamier (if not scatty) the other is likely to become.

It is not only in relationships, however, that dormant potential subpersonalities can be activated. They can be called out with increasing age, especially if the person is especially aware or reflective, or by significant events or traumas. Religious conversion is an example of the sudden awakening of the feeling and intuitive energies in a person who hitherto has been very intellectual or worldly, perhaps even to the point of shallowness or decadence. For Gautama the Buddha, the catalyst was reflection on the realities of life from which his privileged existence in a royal palace had shielded him: poverty, disease, old age and death. For Francis of Assisi, the rich merchant's son, embracing a leper freed his romantic feeling/spirit side from the leather bottle in which his 'down-to-earth' father would imprison it. This transformed him into the most charming Rebellious Son (and enabled him to found the *nicest* religious order) in history. The awakening of intellect and intuition for Ignatius Loyola, the founder of the Jesuits, was rather more drastic: this gallant officer and ladies' man found himself suddenly a cripple when his leg was shattered by a cannon ball and for the first time in his life he was forced to meditate during his long convalescence. It works both ways: men of the world can become monks later in life, priests drop out and marry, austere meditators become Zorbas.

Unexpressed parts of ourselves form much of the stuff of dreams. These potential or denied selves appear to us in disguise when we are asleep. They take form not only as other people, but as places, animals and objects. Everything in our dreams is us; we dream only of our selves. There are several ways of working with dreams with a view to integrating their messages in our lives and freeing buried subpersonalities. One of the most effective ways of doing this is through a technique called Voice Dialogue. The pioneers of this psychotherapeutic technique, Drs Hal Stone and Sidra Winkelman, describe and analyse the following dreams in their Voice Dialogue Manual, *Embracing Our Selves*.

Dream of the hand in the earth

I am walking on a country road. Suddenly I hear a noise; it sounds like a cry. I look down and, to the side of the road, I see a hand sticking up from the earth. I am shocked and I run to the hand and start digging until I unearth the body of a child three or four years of age. He is barely alive. I start to clean him off and I hold him to me.

The dreamer was Ralph, a successful, hardworking, rational man of 62. The authors comment:

In this dream, the awakening comes as an unearthing of something that was buried long ago. It is the Inner Child. Ralph had spent his life identified with parts of himself that pushed him towards great success financially and politically. Something was missing from his life. He had never known real intimacy with others. In this dream he begins to deal with that intimacy as he makes the remarkable discovery that a very important part of himself has been buried. The buried child is the part of himself that carries his vulnerability, his fear of the world, his feelings of isolation and his fear of abandonment. This child was 'buried'. This self was fully repressed at the age of three or four.

It is as if the psyche is constantly seeking to redress one-sided living, favouritism shown by the Ego to certain subpersonalities at the expense of others, as in this dream of Marilyn, a 30-year-old woman who was totally identified with her role as a mother.

Dream of mother identification

Sounds have become acute. There is so much noise and confusion I cannot rest. I finally become fully awake and I look about me. It is as if I were in a strange house and yet I know that it is my house and that I have lived in it for a long time. There is a mirror across from my bed and I glance at it. I am horrified to see that I have grown old while I slept. The noise is deafening and I go out and try to find where it is coming from. As I reach the kitchen door, I realize it comes from there. Around the kitchen table are many people, some young, some older by far than I am. They are all in children's clothes and are waiting to be fed. They see me and begin to pound their bowls on the table and call 'mother' to me. I see my priest across the room with his back to be, and I think surely he can explain this to me, but as I approach him he turns around and I see he is wearing a bib and is holding his bowl too!

I run back to the door to leave and, as I pass the table, I see my parents there, wearing bibs like all the rest. I reach the door as a man comes in. I know him to be my husband, although he is not the husband I had when I went to sleep. He makes a pass at me and I feel relieved, thinking at least he doesn't think I am his mother. When I look at him, however, he is wearing short pants and his face is the face of a child. I think that this is a nightmare and I run and shut myself in my room in order to wake up more fully, but I know I am not asleep. I ask myself over and over again: 'What have I done while I slept?' Ray comes into the room (Ray is a therapist in the city where she lived). I think that surely he can help me to understand this, but he is crying because he has hurt his knee and wants me to bandage it.'

Drs Stone and Winkelman comment:

This dream clearly shows Marilyn's moment of awakening. Until now, the only reality she has known has been the computer program of 'Mother' into which she was locked at an early age. The dream image is so poignant — she has grown old while she slept and, during this sleep, everyone around her has become a child needing nurturing. But now Marilyn is awake and she is separating from her identification with this mother part of herself. She is looking at herself and her surroundings through newly opened eyes and thus beginning to ask questions and to search for something different. She is curious. She wants to discover what exists within her, other than this Mother, and to move toward the fullness of her being.

Our intuitive self, the part of us that 'knows', often appears in dreams as an old man or woman, and usually when the Ego is losing its sense of direction. Drs Stone and Winkelman describe the following example of the Inner Guide appearing to a woman who discovered in her late thirties that she had multiple sclerosis. This dream also suggested that transformation was happening at a deep level in the psyche, represented by the archetype of the Alchemist.

The Old Magician

I am waiting by a dusty roadside. I see an old man approaching far down the road on my left. He carries a heavy pack on his back. When he reaches the place where I am waiting I step into the road to walk with him. The road leads into the forest. After walking deep into the forest we see a small squirrel dart into our path. The old man catches it and cuts it open and removes something from it. I do not see what it is, but the wound is closed quickly by the old man who has hands as sure as a surgeon's. The squirrel is then released.

We go on our way through the forest again. As the sun begins its descent we see a small thatched cottage and enter it. A very old man with a long white beard is in one room that makes up the interior of the cottage. He is sitting in front of a great cooking pot on the hearth. My companion opens his pack and takes from it the object he removed from the squirrel. He hands it to the old man who seems to be a magician. The old magician drops it into his black cooking pot and after a moment it is transformed into a bluebird which flies from the pot. It flies to my travelling companion who places it on my shoulder. I am a little hesitant about resuming my journey alone as I do not know the way, but from time to time the little bird flies on ahead and then returns and shows me the way to go.

Dreams like this one are positive and helpful, pointing us

in new directions if we manage to understand their message. If we can do so, we can bring to birth subpersonalities that are still embryonic, and so enrich our lives. Some dreams, however, are nightmares. In them the dream figures that terrify us are disowned rather than potential selves, parts of us that have been banished to the darkness of the Unconscious because they were unacceptable. There they gather energy and become demonic, rather like a cat that has been shut away in a dustbin. Once the lid is off (when conscious control is switched off during sleep) the creature will emerge like a bat from hell, and understandably so. Being shut in with the rubbish is not a pleasant experience.

But this is what we do with bits of ourself that we have been conditioned to reject as 'bad' or 'ugly'. We think that, because we are no longer aware of them, they no longer exist. But all that has happened is that they have been pushed out of the light of consciousness and become part of the Shadow, our discarded 'rubbish'. Originally they were repressed to safeguard us from outside disapproval by parent figures. The latters' taboos imposed by parents were then internalized to become our Protector-Controller 'conscience' subpersonality, which, as we saw earlier, is the most heavyweight of all the subpersonalities, and the one with which most people identify with and think of as 'them'. But whenever the vigilance of the Protector-Controller is relaxed (as it may be, not only during sleep, but under the influence of drugs like alcohol), the repressed energies have their opportunity to slip out and create mayhem.

We all know the personality changes that happen under the influence of drink, and we met them in Sam. The energies that have been repressed emerge, but they have been too long consigned to the garbage heap, in disturbing or unattractive form, like our poor cat. The drunk's vulnerability when at last allowed to surface can be maudlin, his playfulness aggressive, his sexuality lecherous, his power hostile.

Some of these repressed subpersonalities are instinctual ones to do with aggression and sex. It is right and proper that these powerful energies should be kept under control, for civilized living would be impossible otherwise. But they are better controlled by an aware Ego than by another subpersonality like the Protector-Controller that represses without considering external circumstances or appropriateness. It is very important to note that one does not have to *become* these disowned energies or to act them out in order to integrate them with the rest of the personality. They are content with mere acknowledgement of their existence and respect for their power. Indeed, this is a *sine qua non* for their integration and transformation. By acknowledging their power, crude aggression can be turned into self confidence and strength, blind sex into intimacy and love.

What happens to energies that are disowned? Since energy cannot be destroyed it has to go somewhere. Pushed down into the Unconscious it turns negative and destructive. A disowned subpersonality is like an outcast, behaves like any person who feels rejected and unloved. It has nothing to lose any more and becomes either depressive or rebellious and, sometimes, so recklessly destructive as to merit the term demonic.

A disowned subpersonality haunts us until it is recognized as a part of us with its own song to sing, its own contribution to add to the fullness of our being. It can make us tense, neurotic, ill. Power energies denied become frustration and depression, as aggression is turned inwards: vulnerability unacknowledged breeds paranoia and phobias. Repression, holding down something alive that is trying to get out, takes up a lot of our energy, and is draining. We are unable to truly relax, for our Protector-Controller has to go on holding down the lid lest the monstrous cat escapes. Our well-being suffers together with our quality of life.

The hidden saboteur within us can become as reckless as a kamikaze pilot. There is a well-established correlation between cancer and the habitual repression of emotion, as if cell formation that has gone out of control is a physical manifestation of energy beyond our control. Tracking down a subpersonality that has become self-destructive (demonic?) is now part of the holistic approach to treating cancer patients, together with more orthodox medical treatment. The link between unconscious negative programmes and disease in general is very much part of the holistic approach to health, and may well be an avenue to be explored in coping with the phenomenon of AIDS.

A disowned energy within the unconscious can make us as sick, or at least as uncomfortable, as an undigested meal. It also acts rather like a magnet inside us attracting uncomfortable experiences. We may not be aware of our own negativity but other people will. They will sense the hostility behind the smiling mask of the Pleaser, the Controller posing as Nurturing Parent, the manipulator hidden behind the Victim . . . and either shrink from us, be on their guard, or react. Not seeing the parts of our selves that they sense, we may feel hurt, rejected, resentful that our good intentions go unappreciated . . . But, as we have seen, personal interaction goes beyond the merely verbal: we relate to each other primarily on a subtler energy level. Whatever is unexpressed in you will resonate with a similar energy in me. 'How can I hear what you are saying when what you are is shouting at me?' I may not know why, but I will not feel comfortable in your presence. Unknown to both of us, your disowned subpersonality is activating an energy in me that I do not feel comfortable with.

> I do not love thee, Doctor Fell,
> The reason why I cannot tell;
> But this alone I know full well,
> I do not love thee, Doctor Fell.

But then you will probably not feel comfortable with me either, for Doctor Fell works both ways. Even if I do not in fact pick up your unconscious negativity, you may project it onto me. Your Protector-Controller is not content with keeping the disowned energy at bay within: it is constantly scanning the environment like radar for the same type of energy. Since the Ego is quite unaware that this is happening, its strings will be pulled by the Protector-Controller into believing that the other person is totally unacceptable for any number of very plausible reasons. Better to believe this than to accept the unacceptable: that the other person is the embodiment of an energy that I fear or loathe in myself.

This paranoia of the Protector-Controller is the fuel for persecution in all its forms, and when it becomes a collective phenomenon it gathers to itself a demonic energy that is more frightening than the energy it represses so ferociously could ever be. It zones in on any minority on which it can pin its projected dread of 'contamination', cloaking its real panic with high-sounding slogans. That these usually have a socially cohesive ring — 'racial purity', 'national unity', 'religious orthodoxy', 'sanctity of family life', 'preservation of traditional values/ standard of living' — betrays the fear of disintegration of national or cultural identity on the part of the Protector-Controller-dominated Collective Ego. It is the same as the dread of schizophrenic breakdown felt by the individual Ego.

The sheer relentlessness of those who seek out 'heresy' in all its forms, whether religious, political, sexual or racial, resembles the compulsive handwashing of the obsessional neurotic in dread of accidental contamination, only on a vast scale. Since the shadow is always dark, it follows that its colour will always be blindly associated with anything black by Protector-Controllers whose paranoia has made Ego-intelligence fly out of the window. For too long the darker-coloured peoples of this planet have been saddled with the whiteman's Shadow. But racism will continue as long as we go on using expressions like 'There are black sheep in every flock', 'black as sin' and similar negative associations, including death and mourning.

The racist aspect of the Protector-Controller ignores the elegance of black tulips, dinner jackets, cocktail dresses and Talleyrand's recipe for coffee:

Black as the devil,
Hot as hell,
Pure as an angel,
Sweet as love.

Another problem with repressing (as opposed to controlling) any energy is that it is not available for us to use when we need it. And there are times when we really do need, for example, to have the energy of our Power subpersonalities at our ready disposal for when we are threatened, or when those we love or are responsible for are in danger. Our anger could save our life one day: instant access to our rage at the outrage of being attacked could well scare off an assailant who thought we were easy meat. A woman who has acknowledged her own power will not attract the same unwelcome attentions as her unliberated sister whose unconscious 'helpless female' messages will draw predatory males to her like sharks. A woman who is in touch with her 'Killer' subpersonality, who could kill in self-defence, is perhaps less likely to be raped. 'Something in the way she moves' will warn off a would-be-attacker, for the energies we carry reveal themselves in the way we carry ourselves, in body language. It is well known in cities where mugging is an everyday occurrence (New York, for example) that there is a correlation between one's level of paranoia and the times one gets mugged. Energy finds its own level with unerring exactness: nemesis homes in on its target like a rocket.

It behoves us then to become aware of the hidden energies we are carrying around within us lest they haunt us both within and without — and even when we sleep. Much, if not all, cases of demonic possession or manifestation are more understandable if we think in terms of eruption of repressed and disowned Shadow energies. Does this explain, one wonders, (or merely explain away), the diabolic phenomena that feature so often in the Lives of the Saints: of Saint Anthony of Padua, for example, or the Curé d'Ars? The brighter the light, the more demonic the shadow: the Prince of Darkness, after all, was Lucifer, Bringer of Light (whose overambitious Driver, perhaps, like Icarus', was responsible for his Fall).

These vipers in our bosoms (or rather, our Unconscious) can make us ill, drive us mad or add to the madness in the world. One thing is certain. They will not just go away of their own accord. We have to reclaim these parts of us and honour them too, instead of disowning and projecting them — thereby creating more scapegoats.

MOVIE MYTHS
Archetypes

These energies within us that we have been personifying as subpersonalities in order to understand them better were personified by the ancient Greeks as gods. And, like our subpersonalities, these Gods behaved just like real people. They fell in love, quarrelled over jurisdiction, behaved really quite badly at times. They appear to have been competitive with each other and sensitive to their popularity ratings with devotees. Certainly they were jealous gods, and vengeful if they felt they were being neglected. Though the Greeks might have had a favourite deity, they were careful to honour them all, for they believed the one you did not honour was the one who would 'get you' with one of those awful punishments that only Gods could think up.

Drs Stone and Winkelman quote the story of one such punishment meted out by a jealous God to one who refused to acknowledge him. King Pentheus of Thebes was a devotee of Apollo, who had reigned as a primary deity since the fall of Crete between 1400 and 1000 BC. The King strongly disapproved of the ecstatic and orgiastic rites of the new cult of Dionysus, imported from the North and adopted by some of his subjects (including, unknown to Pentheus, his wife and mother). One night the King had a dream in which Dionysus appeared to him. The god (apparently sober for once) seemed to respect Pentheus' veneration of Apollo, but insisted that the King must also honour Dionysus in some small way. The God added, mysteriously, that if the King would not agree to dance this 'minor dance' to the god, he would have to dance the 'major dance'.

On awakening, furious, the King issued a proclamation banning the cult of Dionysus from his kingdom. That night however was the night of the full moon and a time already arranged for a coming together of the adherents of Dionysus in the forest adjoining the palace. After the King was asleep his wife and mother slipped out of the palace to join in the festivities, already becoming noisy as the wine flowed more freely. Pentheus soon awoke, realized what was happening and, in a blind rage, headed for the Bacchanalian scene to put a stop to it.

As he approached the clearing where it was all happening he was spotted by his mother, who by now was drunk and ecstatic. Mistaking him for a lion (a mistake inspired, no doubt, by Dionysus) she ran him through with her spear. Then, cutting off her son's head, she carried it proudly, impaled on her spear, into Thebes, still believing it to be that of a lion. Thus Pentheus did the 'major dance' of death after all, because he had refused to dance the minor dance of merely honouring the jealous god. Myth though it may be, like all myths that endure, it is grounded in psychological truth: in this case, that any energy that is disowned turns negative and potentially destructive.

Broadly speaking, our subpersonalities could be classified as Apollonian or Dionysian, according to the type of energy they carry. The energy pattern represented by Apollo, god of light, order, harmony, includes all subpersonalities that influence the ego in the direction of structure, control, clarity, rational ways of thinking and acting. The Dionysian pattern predisposes us towards experiencing through the senses, emotional release, the instinctual and the ecstatic.

These energy patterns are innate in us all, primordial psychological instincts that Jung called archetypes. The more layers of subpersonalities one uncovers in oneself, the more archetypal and less purely personal they become: the more one recognizes them outside oneself, not only in other people but in literature, in drama, in myths and fairy tales — and films, the fairy tales of our day. Indeed, the more one can identify with the characters or the action in a movie, the more one feels one has got one's money's worth. That so many people can identify with the same character is possible only if the Collective Unconscious postulated by Jung is indeed a reality. As John Donne expressed it three centuries ago:

> No man is an Island, entire of itself;
> every man is a piece of the Continent,
> a part of the main.

The same types of archetypal energies, bondings and polarizations occur, rehashed to contemporary taste, in the stories enjoyed by each generation. *Plus c á change, plus c'est la même chose*. We are enchanted, thrilled, horrified, moved by this unending Dance of the Archetypal Selves, precisely because we resonate with them, for they are indeed projections onto the cinema or television screen of our own selves, whether potential, disowned or fully-blown indentifications. One of the trivial pursuits of the future may well be trying to figure out afterwards which archetypal strings were being artfully pulled by the movie-maker as we sat, open-mouthed and resonating, totally involved in the archetypal happenings on the big or small screen. Here, to start you off, are a few examples.

ARCHETYPAL POLARIZATIONS

The polarization of Apollonian and Dionysian energies is the basic stuff of all stories in which the 'goodies' fight the 'baddies'. Apollo stands for law and order, and Dionysus for bending or breaking the rules of society, or, in Freudian terms, Superego versus Id. These opposite energies fight it out in many different disguises, and each generation finds new ways of staging the conflict between the two sides.

Cowboys and Indians seem to have had their day, but cops 'n' robbers are here to stay, judging by the perennial popularity of television 'crime series'. The appearance of the Iron Curtain spawned a whole new genre, counter-intelligence versus spies, and the swinging sixties gave rise to the *Easy Rider* type of polarization of straights versus hippies.

Changing social attitudes are reflected in the projection of the Shadow: who exactly are the goodies and who are the baddies? When the distinctions start to become blurred perhaps it is a sign that this particular genre has been overworked and has to make room for a new one. When Indians start to behave as nobly as the Paleface, cops are portrayed as crooked or as violent as the criminals they hunt down, and the latter become as sympathetically kooky as Bonnie and Clyde or Butch Cassidy and Sundance, Dionysus is on top for a while. But only temporarily: they have to die in the end, for 'crime must not be seen to pay' — proof that the social order (by definition) identifies with the Apollonian. Sometimes, surely, in real life, however regrettably, crime does pay. But there is always something disturbing or at least 'unfinished' about a film when the convention of the criminal's comeuppance is disregarded.

Why certain films are wildly successful while others sink without trace is interesting. Dionysus tends to do well at the box office in those periods when there is dissatisfaction with the powers that be, distrust of the controlling or manipulative aspects of Apollonian governments and their agencies, or impatience with repressive attitudes within society. Vietnam, Watergate, the CIA, created a climate of malaise. It spawned films which earlier would have been branded as 'unpatriotic' or 'subversive', in which much of the drama centred around 'cover-ups' by faceless (and therefore scary), devious and uncaring officialdom, as, for example, in *Missing*. Yet this must not be allowed to go too far, for the audience's collective Child's trust in the power of the Governmental Parent to protect it must not be totally undermined. Its heroes, as portrayed for example, by James Bond, or by Michael

Caine in *The Ipcress File* may be Dionysian, but still, reassuringly, they are working for Apollo and backed up in tight spots by his minions, however unsympathetically.

As well as this basic confrontation between Apollonian and Dionysian energies, other archetypes polarize to provide the backgrounds to great epics. The confrontation between Mars and Eros is a recurring theme where a love affair is played out against a background of war, usually with enforced separations, passionate coming together, much soul-searching on the part of the hero as to where his duty lies, and much agonizing by the heroine over virtually everything. One thinks naturally of *Gone With The Wind*, of *Doctor Zhivago*, *War and Peace*, but also of the feud-cross'd lovers in *Romeo and Juliet* and *West Side Story*.

GODDESSES

For a whole generation Hollywood became a shrine to Aphrodite. It created one image of the Love Goddess after another: Jean Harlow, Rita Hayworth, Hedy Lamar, Lana Turner, Ava Gardner . . . Seductive as sirens yet as unattainable as stars, they made fortunes for their studios by allowing themselves to be the recipients of anima-projection by men and projective identification by their women fans. The story of one such anima-projection, *The Blue Angel*, in fact started the career of Marlene Dietrich, the most perennial of these Love Goddesses. Their elusive quality was epitomized in Garbo, whose famous 'I want to be alone' underlined the Goddess's need to distance herself from these mortal projections in order not to be toppled off her pedestal by them.

The last of them was Marilyn Monroe, whose Vulnerable Child suffocated to death under the heavy mink mantle of the Love-Goddess she was asked to be in real life, as well as to play on the screen. It was not only her tragedy that dethroned Aphrodite from her pre-eminence as the Ideal Woman. With the advent of the women's movement a new Goddess was claiming adherents — Athena. This female combination of the energies of Apollo and Mars provided women with a new model of awareness and militant independence. It created as much confusion and disarray in the male camp as this formidable Protectress of Athens had occasioned to the Persians and Spartans who dared to challenge her supremacy in the fifth century BC. Once again, films, the richest sources for future writers of the history of our century, reflected the trend in the new breed of intelligent, tough divas carrying the energy of Athena: Jane Fonda, Vanessa Redgrave, Diane Keaton, Jessica Lange . . .

When this energy is combined with that of the Fixer we get the Bitch-Goddess, as played by Bette Davis in many films, but most memorably perhaps in *The Little Foxes*. That the charisma of Joan Collins as Alexis Colby makes *Dynasty* seem less plastic whenever she is in a scene might be explained by the fact that she embodies so many archetypal energies that, in comparison, the other characters seem one-dimensional. In Alexis the power of Athena, the seductiveness of Aphrodite, the fierce protectiveness of the Controlling Mother are allied to the devious manipulativeness of the Fixer — a truly awesome combination.

ARCHETYPAL BONDINGS

The interplay of the male and female archetypal energies lends itself to a vast number of possible combinations, from the frankly pornographic, through stereotypical 'boy meets girl' encounters, to more sophisticated interpersonal interactions. Bondings which include the natural tension between Apollonian and Dionysian energies enliven the relationship, as do those between Jung's opposite Psychological Types. As usually happens, the protagonists' increased tolerance and understanding of each other by the end is warmly satisfying, at one level almost healing, for the audience. *African Queen, The Lion in Winter, My Fair Lady, The Sound of Music* were, from this point of view, variations on the same theme. Eros here yields place to the mock asexual battle between Apollonian and

Dionysian-dominated Egos to provide the main action, which is why you could take your maiden aunt (or your school party) to see *The Sound of Music* without qualms, even though it was a love story. The archetypal fascination of the theme could even be carried over into portraying intense relationships man-to-man or woman-to-woman without incurring the wrath of the anti-gay lobby (or, much more to be feared, box-office death) in such successful films as *Midnight Cowboy, Butch Cassidy and the Sundance Kid, Zorba the Greek, Julia* and *Black Widow*.

These are just a few examples of recurring archetypal bondings that we all find easy to relate to, which is why, of course, film-makers keep using them. Occasionally they treat us to a one-off original bonding patterns rather than serving up the fixed and familiar ones in new dress, putting their money this time on the public's insatiable appetite for novelty as well as on its equally insatiable need to 'project onto' or 'identify with'. In the novelty category come the Elsas-and-Lassies-plus-human types of bondings, nuns and cowboys, princesses and newspapermen, transvestites and showgirls, whores and chauffeurs *ad infinitum*.

HEROES

The hero archetype must undergo great ordeals, preferably voluntarily, in the service of an ideal, or, more usually, an Ideal Woman. He must triumph over the odds heavily loaded against him: the more apparently insuperable they are, the greater his heroic status. The Anti-Hero briefly in vogue in the heyday of Women's Lib broke all these conventions, sometimes to great comic effect, as in *The Graduate*. But Anti-Hero is not an archetype with the power of the Rebel (as played by Brando) or Rebellious Son, who, as James Dean, remains a Hero today, long after his death, for many young people. The Hero archetype allows for several different clearly-defined subpersonalities in type-casting without breaking the heroic mould.

These include the Romantic, the Warrior, the Adventurer, the Saviour.

As with the Love Goddesses, the heyday of the Great Lover in the Rudolph Valentino/Clark Gable tradition is past. And so, perhaps, post-Vietnam, is that of the Warrior as exemplified in the stengun- and grenade-toting heroes of the host of military epics spawned by World War II. However, the phenomenon of *Rambo*'s brute violence (and, even more unnerving, its enthusiastic reception in high places) would seem to suggest that this may not be so. Today's Warrior must still be able to fight (preferably with his fists and judo or karate as well as with firearms), but his adversaries are more likely to be street muggers or hostile invaders from the skies (another indication of contemporary anxieties). But that there is still room for the swashbuckling Adventurer, Douglas Fairbanks/Errol Flynn style, was shown by the success of *Raiders of the Lost Ark*, though this also pointed up the fact that, for today's more sophisticated tastes, the picaresque can only be served up to audiences tongue-in-cheek if they are not to fall about laughing in the aisles, or start hissing the villain.

The Hero archetype most acceptable to us today would seem to be the Saviour. In film after film this archetype saves the rest of the cast from perils which range from an assortment of monsters (now in danger of extinction through over-exposure) to assorted disasters like blazing infernos, highjacks, plane crashes, the threat of nuclear war, or space invaders. Or tyranny and injustice, if one thinks of *Gandhi*, a Saviour with the added charisma of the Wise Man/Good Father archetypes.

That the Saviour is an archetypal subpersonality is neatly underlined in the *Superman* series. Our Hero periodically doffs the cape and long-johns which are the Saviour uniform in favour of the horn-rims which tell us immediately that he has switched roles and is now in his intellectual mode. The Hero of who-dunnits could also be considered to embody the Saviour since he spares the audience having to witness any more grisly murders than it absolutely has to, notably when the Killer tries to strike again in the last reel. Thriller writers have to make him Apollonian so he can get on with the job of sorting out the clues. In performing this task he has to be able to draw on intuition as well as reasoning power, thus combining 'Saviour' with a dash of 'Rational Man' and 'Knower of Secrets'. (Perhaps Agatha Christie's success was due not only to her ingenious plots but to her originality in making Hercule Poirot also a Dionysian and making her most popular Hero-Saviour a little old lady. But then, if actor-cowboys can make it to President, anything must be possible.)

THE CHILD ARCHETYPE

Cartoon characters are almost invariably Child archetypes, and certainly Walt Disney must have had much of Magical Child in him to have created so many. Much of the action in cartoons is to do with the inventiveness of the Playful Child which often goes so much 'over the top' as to be positively sadistic, as in the Tom and Jerry, Bugs Bunny 'bash-about' variety. This is war on a playpen fantasy level in which, since none of the characters can get really hurt, all is fair. They get blown up by sticks of dynamite, squashed flat by grand pianos, cut up into segments — but always manage to pull themselves together ready for the next round. The least childlike of them all is Donald Duck, who is usually more a combination of Controller, Driver and Victim, while Micky Mouse, on the other hand, has a much more developed Pleaser.

Some of the classic Disney full-length features follow the fairy-tale themes along the archetypal lines of Hansel and Gretel and are about the perils encountered by the Vulnerable Child in a Cruel World. The Child is sometimes represented by a young animal, for example Bambi and Dumbo being ill-treated by witches (Bad Mothers), sorcerers (Bad Fathers), and scowling trees with clutching branches (an unsupportive environment). Distinctions between Good and Evil are always black and white, and Good always triumphs in the end, with the aid of cuddly chipmunks, inventive squirrels and twittering birds. The archetypal Babe in the Wood is Snow White, whose innocence is so extreme that it has to be balanced by seven dwarfs (with names suggestive of subpersonalities), rather like Cinderella who needs her Ugly Sisters around to keep her grounded. Both girls, of course, must get their Prince in the end, and live happily ever after. Vulnerable Child is often seen possessing some of the attributes of Magical Child, and usually wanting to find its way back home after getting lost. Such were *Pinocchio* and Spielberg's *ET*, whose alienation and longing for Good Parent and 'home' respectively, powerful symbols of the need to belong, resonated with the Lost Child in us all. As did *The Wizard of Oz*.

THE SHADOW

The money-making potential of the collective Shadow has long been exploited by moviemakers in the form of horror films carefully designed to resonate with it. Judging by the perennial popularity of the genre, they have done their psychology homework well.

Since we sense that these slumbering subhuman subpersonalities in our Shadow can be reanimated at any time (*Frankenstein* and derivatives), we expend so much energy trying to keep them down that we could become drained (*Dracula, Night of the Living Dead* and derivatives). Constant vigilance is required lest the monster lurking in the depths of our unconscious should rise to the surface and destroy our identity with cold savagery (*Jaws* and derivatives). That so many of the horrific images are beasts of some kind acknowledges the instinctual nature of much of the repressed material in the unconscious. That disowned aggression and sexuality form much of the contents of the Collective Shadow (and that filmmakers are mainly men) explains why monsters always seem to be mainly after the girl. Indeed, as in the classic 'girl-meets-ape' bonding of Fay Wray and *King Kong*, they can even, apparently, get quite a crush . . . More violent, however, than King Kong are the psychopaths in *Psycho, Dressed to Kill, Hallowe'en* and derivatives. This type of film is particularly disturbing because it taps into the Ego's fear of going mad as well as of sudden and violent death.

The more Apollonian and orderly the Ego, the more anarchic and Dionysian its Shadow. Within the bounds allowed by film censorship, unrestrained sexual licence as well as blasphemous idolatry are suggested in the 'black magic' type of film. The leader of the coven is always high-placed, wealthy, owns a mansion furnished with antiques, is usually suave, well-spoken and something of a connoisseur. This appeals to the audience's collective Driver's lust for earthly riches, leisure and status — or it may be considered another black mark against the villain. Either way, the affluent lifestyle of this devilish villain conveys the idea of decadence more effectively than if he were portrayed having to clock in at work every morning like the rest of us.

More disturbing though, is when the Shadow is linked with the Child archetype, particularly in stories of demonic possession or strange powers, as in *The Exorcist, The Omen, Rosemary's Baby, Carrie* and their like. Such perversion of the Child Archetype's energies of vulnerability, playfulness and innocence is particularly disturbing because it resonates with the long-forgotten destructive fantasies of our own Omnipotent Child.

IDENTITY AND TRANSFORMATION

The suspicion that characters may not always be what they present themselves to be provides much of the suspense in mystery and 'psychological' thrillers, as, for example, in *Sleuth, Deathtrap, Les Diaboliques* and, of course, who-dunnits. This genre has an appeal for the Intellectual puzzle-solver and lacks the crude violence and blood-letting of horror movies designed purely to numb the audience with shock. Not to be sure as to who is telling the truth, who can be trusted and who cannot, what is real and what isn't, is endlessly fascinating because it resonates with the uncertainties and insecurities most of us experience from time to time in real life. It is always something of a shock (as well as a relief) when the real murderer is unmasked, especially if we have been encouraged all the way through to identify with him or her.

When the villain actually peels off a mask to reveal that all the time he has been someone else, there is usually a perceptible *frisson* among the audience. One wonders whether this resonates with our need to keep our own *persona* firmly in place, and how naked and threatened we would feel if we too were thus brusquely unmasked, the way we like to present ourselves in the world shown up to be a brave deception (even worse, a self-deception). It would be more fun to assume different identities, to *choose* which of them you want to be and to don that sub-personality with the mask and the costume. This is not only what carnivals and fancy dress parties are about, but why they generate higher energy than other social functions where people are afraid to step out of their every-day roles. Self-expression is naturally more exuberant than self-concealment.

Dr Jekyll kept his Shadow Mr Hyde, like an evil genie, in a phial in his laboratory, Dorian Gray's Shadow, the portrait of an extremely ugly old man, was hidden in the attic. This type of film is about Transformation. Once it starts it is hard to stop, as any werewolf (or psychoanalyst) will tell you. Psychoanalysts will also tell you that the process of transformation can be painful, but, once you come out the other end, you discover you have energies at your disposal that you did not have before. And you see yourself and others differently. This is what happened not only to Mr Hyde and the werewolves, but to the Ugly Duckling, the frogs who finally managed to get kissed by a princess, and Eliza Doolittle.

PULLING YOUR OWN STRINGS
The aware ego

Models of the aware Ego

- an effective, democratic Prime Minister
- a good host
- a charioteer

All the world's a stage,
And all the men and women merely players;
They have their exits and their entrances;
And one man in his time plays many parts.
Shakespeare

In the preceding chapters we have been looking at some of the parts people play habitually throughout their lives. These parts, which together help to make up their personalities we called subpersonalities. In this final chapter we will look at the Player of these parts, the Consciousness that has the intelligence, the capacity to be aware of the role it is playing *as well as playing it*. This conscious, as opposed to unconscious, part of ourselves which Freud called the Ego, may be more or less aware of itself at any one time, just like an actor on stage, depending on how deeply immersed he is in the role. Whether he forgets it or not, the actor's objective reality is that he is the player, not the part. In living out our daily existence, we, too, could forget that we are more than just the sum total of our parts or subpersonalities, but this is not exactly a blueprint for quality in life. At worst, if we are unlucky, such forgetfulness on the part of the Ego can breed isolation, desperation, or mental and physical illness.

Feeling identified with any subpersonality, 'stuck with yourself' (or what you assume is 'you'), feeling driven by inner tensions or pulled apart by them, impelled to act them out — this is what is meant by having your strings pulled. The more you are aware of the part you are playing, the easier it is to keep your act together. You will not let it run away with you.

NON-IDENTIFICATION

To be identified with any particular part of us is to be like an actor who not only plays Hamlet, but actually thinks he is the Prince of Denmark. The disadvantages of this identification (let alone its nightmarishness) should be obvious. Trapped in the role, he is doomed to go on repeating it over and over again: he has given himself no choice to be, or not to be Hamlet. Or, indeed, to play any other part — which makes him in the end boring and predictable. He will cease to develop as an actor, he will fail to discover his range and his limits, to learn from experiencing other roles and dramatic interaction. Stuck with Hamlet, he will also be stuck with the cast and the plot that goes with the role, the set of experiences that go with it. Worst of all, off-stage, the effects of acting out a part for which the stage has not been set, will make people view him as mad. He is a victim of his own lack of awareness. Unless somehow he becomes aware of his freedom to step out of role any time he chooses, the part will continue to run his life as if he were a puppet on a string. If he gains this new awareness, however, he can go on playing Hamlet, or not: he now has a choice which he did not have before. The part no longer controls him; he *plays* it.

We are talking here, of course, about the relationship of the Ego to the subpersonalities we have been describing. The Inner Child, Parent, Pleaser, Critic and so on. All of them, as we have seen, have something to offer us — providing they are kept in their rightful place. Indeed, not to allow them their rightful place is asking for trouble. Subpersonalities, however useful as servants, make poor masters of the house; they don't care about the other residents and think only of getting their own needs met. To have overall vision, to assess the appropriateness of the often importunate demands of the more vociferous or persuasive subpersonalities, to listen for the softer voices of less strident but wiser parts of us, and then to act on the basis of priority, appropriateness and common interest — this is the job of the Ego, not of any one subpersonality.

Society expects us to take responsibility for what we do with these energies inside us, and disapproves or punishes if we do not. Several models usefully express this responsible position of the Ego *vis-à-vis* the subpersonalities. It could be compared with an impartial and effective chairman who draws on the contributions of the members of his board while reserving to himself the final decision; a charioteer who keeps hold of the reins so as to steer the energies of the team of horses in the direction *he*, not they, wishes to go; or a hitherto sleeping host awakening to the fact that some of his guests are getting above themselves while others are feeling threatened and neglected — and again taking charge of his own party so that everybody feels included.

The more aware this 'I' becomes, the less it allows itself to be taken over completely by and identified with the thoughts and feelings fed into it by whichever subpersonality is in the ascendant at any one time, and the less it is likely to be stampeded into one-sided decision making or rash acting-out. Heightened ego-awareness gives us more space to manoeuvre, more sensitivity to timing and appropriateness, more real options for initiating and exploring instead of dull repetition of old habits.

CONFLICT RESOLUTION

The subpersonalities model allows for the easier resolution of conflicts, both inner and outer, making for less tension and unhappiness, blaming and self-blame, guilt and guilt-slinging. The Ego caught in a nutcracker between Superego and Id, Apollonian and Dionysian, Child and Parent or any other pair of polarizing energies no longer has to take sides or be crushed between them. Through knowledge of these selves and non-identification with any one of them, it can view the conflict from the position of the sympathetically impartial and objective observer, rather than from the vastly more uncomfortable one of being impaled on the horns of the dilemma.

'Knowledge itself is power', wrote Bacon — and self-knowledge brings home the bacon in that in empowers the Ego to move from the position of victim of inner conflict to arbitrator. One gives each of these inner belligerents a fair hearing, then decides where justice to each lies — or postpones any decision until more evidence is forthcoming. In the latter case, the Ego is able now to hold the tension of the opposites, to wait with greater patience for a creative resolution of inner conflict to suggest itself, perhaps in a dream, rather than surrendering too easily to the string-pulling of whichever subpersonality is temporarily in the ascendant. It will resist being driven to act out or 'act in', or swinging wildly between the opposites in a manic-depressive way.

In close relationships, the more the partners are able to recognize their own and each other's subpersonalities when these are taking over, the more they will be able to avoid serious quarrels or to settle them more speedily. When mutual irritation is escalating into recrimination and counter-recrimination, the retreat into increasingly entrenched and well-defended polarized positions can be halted. It only needs one of the partners to resist the string-pulling subpersonalities that are running wild to bring some awareness to the *process* of the quarrel rather than its actual *content*.

This means looking behind what is being said, beyond what started the quarrel, to what it is *really about. In most cases, it will be about hurt feelings.* To acknowledge that one or the other partner's Child is feeling threatened is an unthreatening short cut through the defences, attacks or smoke-screens being erected by other subpersonalities that are rallying to defend its vulnerability. The Child, if it feels seen, can now ask directly for the reassurance it needs instead of throwing a tantrum. Similarly, the partner who has been polarized into heavy Controlling Parent will no longer feel obliged to lay down the law if he or she now perceives a Vulnerable Child rather than a Rebellious Son or Daughter. Seeing more clearly what is really happening between them makes continued blind quarrelling impossible. With this awareness the dynamic changes: the partners will now bond rather than polarize, perhaps along the lines of Vulnerable Child/Nurturing-Protecting Parent (cuddles, holding and reassurances), Rational Adults (objective discussion of needs, expectations or house rules), or (perhaps best of all) Playful Children, in which case they 'make up', may have a pillow fight, chase each other, giggling, around the room, and end up making love.

SELF-ACCEPTANCE

The more we can allow ourselves to drop our identification with a certain way of being, the less we will find ourselves plagued by its opposite energy fighting for recognition in the interests of the psyche's balance and wholeness. The more one acknowledges the existence of these Shadow energies in oneself, the less shocked one is by them and the less judgemental. Instead of shrinking from the ugliness of these Calibans or Mr Hydes within us, we begin to become curious about them, and want to know how they got to be 'mis-shapen beasts' in the first place, and what exactly fuels their rage. Instead of continuing to distort these energies and turn them negative or even demonic by repression (as we have been conditioned to do with our selfishness, anger, jealousy, pride etc), or, by acting them out, cause guilt or social repercussions, we try rather to understand 'what makes them tick'.

Once a rogue subpersonality is acknowledged as part of us, welcomed back into the family by the Aware Ego like the Prodigal Son by his father, the nightmare ceases. Other subpersonalities more Superego-orientated will no doubt have opinions and, like the Prodigal Son's older brother, rumble their disapproval — but they have a right to a voice also, for there are many mansions in their father's house, and enough room for all his sons. But there will no longer be any room in us for the self-loathing and self-destructiveness that deepens the Shadow when we are too identified with the light. Too often, the Light we identify with is not the True Light but the Superego. It can pose as the Aware Ego, obscuring the fact that its strings are simply being pulled by the Controller or the Critic.

TRANSFORMATION

The 'True Light' that alone has the power to dispel the darkness of our Shadow is that of Awareness and Love. They go together as inevitably as the wings of a dove, for *tout comprendre, c'est tout pardonner*. Since 'love' is the most misused word in the language, perhaps it will be more meaningful to use another word with the connotation of 'non-judgemental' or allowing someone to be just as they are — with acceptance, respect, and compassion. Getting to know our subpersonalities means, that instead of standing over some of them with finger raised in admonition or hands raised in horror, we are bringing some awareness to understanding them all.

The deeper the self-awareness we cultivate, the more self-acceptance we allow, the more whole we become as we are healed of internal division. For when our consciousness changes, the way energy is constellated in the Unconscious starts to change just as surely as physical changes start to happen in our body – and 'miracles' of healing can happen. Subpersonalities start to add their weight to the body politic rather than sabotaging it, to pull together rather than trying to pull us apart. The energy wasted in the past on repression, conflict, guilt is now available for living, together with the integrated energies of hitherto disowned parts of us. Not only do we experience more well-being through higher energy, relief from tension and a more positive self-image, but our transformed negativity no longer attracts negativity from the outside world. Owning and taking responsibility for our own 'stuff', we no longer need to project it on to others, and with the removal of these motes in our own eyes, clear relating becomes possible at last.

Just as our relationships mirror us, the macrocosm of the world reflects the dynamics and the drama of the Ego's relationship to its subpersonalities. Apollonian and Dionysian energies are today polarized and in conflict at all levels, producing urban violence at home and wars abroad. The more repression, the more terrorism; the more terrorists, the more repression. The Shadow turns demonic in response to the blinding light, which the Controller turns on it with a view to destroying it. The sheer rage that manifests in various forms today in the world is Caliban's rage at seeing his own face in the glass.

From time to time hopes of de-polarization through dialogue are held out by individuals channelling archetypal Saviour energies powerful enough to fascinate the media. Too often these hopes have been dashed, for these Saviours proved lacking, either in enough all-embracing and impartial love to make everybody feel included, or in enough awareness to avoid being assassinated by those who felt left out. Those Saviours who survive too often fall into the trap of identifying with the archetypal energies coming through them. Their Ego-inflation can easily be mistaken for true enlightenment by their followers, whom they then can lead like sheep in the direction of Utopias which are really slaughter-houses. Mercifully, such false Saviours tend to be burnt out eventually by the high-voltage energy they channel without awareness.

What the world needs most of today are not more Saviours, or more Heroes, but more Aware Egos. Transformation of the demonic energies on this planet will only come about when global consciousness has evolved sufficiently for the collective Shadow to be understood, and understood to be everybody's responsibility.

The Aware Ego is a more useful model for us in the West to aim at than the notoriously elusive, ego-eclipsing 'enlightenment' or nirvana of the East. It is also a model for governments, for handling tensions within society and for relating to foreign governments without either jingoistic ego-inflation or paranoia, or risking the psychosis of war. To be able to contain the tension of the opposites; to tolerate differences; to honour all energies and make a place for them, not only the most powerful and therefore the most privileged; to understand minorities and their needs and thus create fewer outcasts and rebels; to facilitate the return of its Prodigal Sons; to be watchful and in charge, but at the same time nurturing and compassionate: these are the hallmarks of a Government that is aware, caring and has 'got its act together' – and, indeed, of any truly civilized society. But if de Maistre is correct in his observation that every nation has the government it deserves, we have all first to work at developing an Aware Ego that relates to its subpersonalities in an accepting, caring way, for real transformation of society happens at grass roots level. And, in this ongoing process of learning to pull our own strings, we also help our neighbours to get off the hook if only because we see them clearly, not merely as our own projections.

APPENDIX
Dialoguing subpersonalities

Self-knowledge can come with growing older, with self-acceptance and maturity. But, unlike physiological growth and biological ageing, the development of an Aware Ego is not an automatic process. Subpersonalities, once firmly established as part of our make-up, may continue throughout our lives to pull our strings as predictably as clockwork unless, for one reason or another, it begins to dawn on our Ego that it is not master of its own house — and decides it is about time it was. Lest you be left with a sinking feeling at the apparent unattainability of such an Aware Ego, here are a few notes on some of the well-established pathways to becoming more self-aware and more self-accepting.

Much Controller-orientated 'religious' education holds up ideal ways of behaving with nary a clue as to how, with the best will in the world, a new state of awareness can possibly be attained. This is tantamount to exhorting people to join one on the roof without first pointing out the ladder. 'Goodness' is not needed in order to raise one's level of consciousness. More awareness is: and goodness, inner harmony and harmlessness to one's fellows are merely the expression of this higher awareness, lived out in our lives and relationships.

What do we have to become more aware of? The motes in the Ego's eyes, the processes of identification, denial and projection that have been described in the preceding chapters. These are the blind spots that effectively conceal our true selves from us and thus enable them to do their own thing in our confusion and discomforture and, sometimes, shame and guilt. 'Identification', claimed Gurdjeiff, 'is the only sin' — and I have suggested a few examples of how identifying with one subpersonality turns it into a heavyweight that can not only throw its weight around the psyche like a bull in a china shop, but bullies the selves of other people as well.

Much of psychotherapy is about the gradual withdrawal of projections. Freud and Jung both agreed that understanding the transference (the client's projections onto the therapist) was at the heart of the therapeutic process; so is reclaiming the Shadow, in the Individuation process. The end of therapy comes when the client's Ego has been empowered to 'go it alone' and is able to pull its own strings, handle its subpersonalities instead of being driven by them. This happens when the Ego has allowed the symptom-producing Prodigal Sons back into the fold (awareness), rather than keeping them out in the cold (unconsciousness). This is facilitated by the therapist's 'unconditional positive regard' for *whichever* subpersonality puts in an appearance during a session, and positive encouragement especially to the Shadow to emerge from the wings (though it has been known, in more cathartic therapy sessions, to make its entrance rather more dramatically, like the Demon King through the stage trap door). As always, awareness and acceptance are the healing, 'whole-making', catalysts, and with the introjection of the analyst's Nurturing Parent, the client carries his own therapist inside him henceforth.

Jung foreshadowed the later personalization of 'complexes' by humanistic psychology by naming archetypes: the Child, the Hero, the Wise Man, for example. But it has been in this generation that therapists have begun to see the value of treating *all* psychic energies as people inside us, a model developed by Fritz Perls in Gestalt, Assagioli in Psychosynthesis, Eric Berne in Transactional Analysis. All of these have evolved techniques for contacting various parts of us and drawing them out (and, as in Gestalt art or Psychosynthesis, literally drawing them, too) in order to see them more clearly and to integrate them.

Each of these approaches has its specialities among subpersonalities. Perls made his reputation at Esalen (the world's first 'growth centre' at Big Sur, California), by exteriorizing and stage-managing with a showman's panache the inner dog-fight going on all the time between the yea-sayer and the nay-sayer in us all. Before the fascinated eyes of Gestalt group participants, Perls would have the 'top dog' and the 'underdog' of a group member confront each other verbally, their host shifting between the two cushions representing the combatants and giving alternately a voice to each. What was so amazing was the *articulateness* of these inner voices, of which the person's Ego had been perhaps unaware until then. Each subpersonality was clear as to what it wanted, would often complain at never having been allowed expression in the person's lifestyle, and would even describe with some glee its stratagems for manipulating its host's Ego to get its needs met, or to sabotage projects which it felt were not in its own interests. By the end of the session, a compromise might have been reached by the polarized subpersonalities (conflict resolution), but if not, at least the person would return to the group with a more Aware Ego.

Eric Berne's bestselling *Games People Play* meant that many of us came to recognize perhaps for the first time, the nature of the intrapsychic energies that stop us behaving like Aware Egos. In Transactional Analysis the Aware Ego would be called the 'Adult'. The clarity of its interactions with other Adults would often be clouded (or, on a bad day, contaminated) by the intrusion of the energies of either Parent or Child. What made for illuminating (and sometimes hilarious) reading were the permutations of bonding and polarizing that manifest when these two subpersonalities (and their offspring) get together or fight it out.

But the games subpersonalities play are often not so

funny. I remember a chilling moment in a Transactional Analysis weekend group when one participant became alerted to why he had been accident-prone all his life, something that had always puzzled him. One of his subpersonalities had in early life, completely logically, given the circumstances at the time, concluded that the best way to ensure being loved was to hurt yourself. He had been carrying around this internal 'script', like a concealed time-bomb, ever since, and acting it out with a succession of 'accidents', each more serious than the last. One wonders just how often our Vulnerable Child, when feeling particularly insecure, makes us fall ill in adult life because it got the message at some stage that concern, caring and attention are more forthcoming when it is having a bad time than when it is being noisily playful. What we tell ourselves is supremely important, for these statements are the seeds from which subpersonalities sprout.

It would seem that lessons we learn (and then forget we ever did) pass into our mind-computers and remain there unchanged as such blueprints for living until the Ego reprogrammes itself. Readers interested specifically in tracking down any negative programmes carried by their subpersonalities could well investigate not only Transactional Analysis, but also the reprogramming techniques offered by Neuro-Linguistic Programming (NLP).

A new technique from America for working with our subpersonalities that is becoming increasingly recognized in Europe is Voice Dialogue. Evolved by ex-Jungian analyst Dr Hal Stone and his wife Dr Sidra Winkelman, it combines elements of all the approaches mentioned above (plus a dash of Moreno's Psychodrama) into a deceptively simple, yet very sophisticated tool for enhancing Ego Awareness. The essence of this approach is to give each subpersonality a voice, to listen to what it has to tell us, and to engage it in dialogue to find out more about it, how this energy is operating in our lives, and what it needs from us.

Exactly how one can do this for oneself will be learned initially by working with a Voice Dialogue facilitator who has been trained to recognize when a different energy is wanting to have a say. Certain kinds of questions are asked to encourage the subpersonalities to emerge more clearly from their home in the unconscious and to speak to us. This they will not do if they feel in any way judged or disapproved of: if there is any hint of disapproval or attempt at manipulation on the part of the facilitator, a subpersonality will shut up and disappear with disconcerting abruptness. This is a built-in safeguard in Voice Dialogue against any manipulation (with the best intentions) on the part of the facilitator in the direction of conflict resolution (as happens so often, one sometimes feels, in Gestalt therapy), or any attempt to persuade a 'negative' subpersonality to 'behave itself'. As we have seen, it is being on the receiving end in the past of so many similar judgements that has turned the subpersonality 'negative' in the first place. For transformation to happen, what it needs is not more judgements, but understanding and acceptance. Voice Dialogue is about allowing our selves to be, exactly as they are, and when, thus encouraged, they explain why they are the way they are, we get to understand why, given their experience, they could not have developed any other way.

By 'we' of course, is meant the Ego, which has been listening all the time its subpersonalities have been singing their song. By the end of the session the Ego is that much more aware of the dynamics at work in the unconscious. Voice Dialogue sessions invariably begin and end with the Ego: the facilitator starts by asking us, perhaps, what we would like to work on, or simply to say what is going on in our lives that needs clarifying. As we talk, one subpersonality will start to come through loud and clear: it may be the plaintive voice of our Hurt Child, the self-castigation of our Critic, the complaints of our Driver that there is never time to get everything done, the Adventurer fed up with our boring job who wants to get away from it all.

At this point, to help make the Ego aware that it is being taken over by a subpersonality, the facilitator will ask the person being facilitated to move physically to another chair and carry on talking from there, thus leaving the vacated Ego space (the chair the person started off the session sitting in) as a silent witness to the revelations of the emerging subpersonality. The subpersonality now holding forth will be encouraged to say more about itself, especially about why it is coming up in the person's life at this time and the energy that is activating and motivating it. Listening to it, one learns a great deal about one's real needs, about priorities, about why one did what one did, when one did. Most valuable of all, identification with this particular subpersonality or polarization against it will no longer be possible, for, as it in turn makes way for other subpersonalities to emerge in the course of the session, it is seen to be only a part of us, and therefore seen in perspective.

A session of Voice Dialogue can be not only an enlightening, ever-fresh experience, but also a dramatic one. As each subpersonality says its piece (always from a different chair), the voice changes, the expression, body posture . . . When Victim is talking one would think, with its complaining and despondency, that the end of the world was at hand. Suddenly a lighter energy starts to shine through the gloom: Victim's voice starts to trail off as another subpersonality wants to take over . . . The facilitator, trained to watch for this, thanks Victim for sharing, asks the person to move to another chair and lo! — there is Playful Child beaming and swinging its legs, prattling on about things it most enjoys doing.

A session ends with the Ego re-instated on the chair it started off on, grounding itself again in the outer reality by discussing with the facilitator the subpersonalities that came up in the course of the session, and what they had to say. No attempt is made to give advice or to resolve any conflicts between subpersonalities that have been highlighted. This would in fact be a subtle disempowerment of the Ego. As it eyes the now empty chairs that a few minutes ago were occupied by its selves and remembers what they said, the Ego has enough information to go on to make its own decisions, based on priority and considerations of objective reality. No attempt, similarly, is made to 'convert' erring subpersonalities: this would merely strengthen the Protector-Controller (which often masquerades as an Aware Ego) in its attempts to suppress them, and drive them further underground. The self-regulating nature of the psyche ensures that transformation, by assimilation, of the Shadow will happen once the Ego acknowledges these disowned parts. Perhaps this will happen in dreams. Voice Dialogue works with dreams in the same way, inviting each component of the dream in turn to identify itself as a subpersonality and to talk about itself. Readers interested in learning more about Voice Dialogue should read Dr Stone and Dr Winkelman's Voice Dialogue manual entitled *Embracing our Selves* (published by New World Library, P.O. Box 13257, Northgate Station San Raphael California 94913, which also lists a contact address for anyone interested in learning to use the method for themselves.

These are some of the awareness techniques so far evolved for getting to know our selves better which you might like to follow up. I have had the pleasure of meeting many of the subpersonalities described in this book both in the course of my own personal growth and in helping, professionally, to facilitate that of others. This is not to suggest that you, too, may not have met all or some of these subpersonalities before, or that you have to be in therapy to meet them. They are manifesting in our lives all the time, from moment to moment, in our moods and in our relationships. Whenever we are talking to somebody, more often than not we are engaging a subpersonality. It has even been suggested that, whenever two people go to bed together, they may think they are alone, but in fact they have taken their Parents and Children into bed with them. A sobering thought.

Of further interest

COMING ALIVE

Louis Proto

Wake up feeling GOOD every day of your life. This is the invitation Louis Proto extends to us all in this unique do-it-yourself manual for coming alive spiritually, mentally and physically. The emphasis throughout is on practical exercises and techniques that can be fitted into even the busiest of daily routines yet DO bring real and lasting beneficial results. He discusses in an easy and informal manner:

- Throwing out negativity
- Body awareness
- Diet and relaxation
- Meditation
- Self diagnosis
- Creative visualization
- Yoga and reflexology
- Massage

TAKE CHARGE OF YOUR LIFE

Louis Proto

A sparklingly witty and deliciously irreverent side-swipe at the excuses all of us present for failure — 'They made me', 'If you'd had the life I've had', 'I don't know what I've done to deserve this'. Louis Proto makes us *laugh* at our extensive capacity for insisting upon our martyrdom, then shows us — in the same good natured and positive way — how we can step out of the role of 'victim' into a bright new tomorrow full of sunshine and reward.

BRING OUT THE MAGIC IN YOUR MIND

Al Koran

Money! Stacks of it! Wads of crisp notes and bags of shining silver – believe and they're yours. Al Koran exposes the unseen powers *that already exist* in your own mind and gives full explanations on how YOU can harness them. Make the magic of your mind work for you to bring you prosperity, success, health, vitality, good looks . . . in fact everything you've ever wanted . . . automatically! *Bring Out The Magic In Your Mind* by Al Koran – your key to the door of limitless success.